SIMPLY ITALIAN, SIMPLY GLUTEN FREE

Mostly plant-based, mostly milk-free, low lactose and lactose-free recipes

by

Anna Del Conte

and

Michelle Berriedale-Johnson

Published in 2020 by Curlew Books

Edited by Sally Beck

Designed by Emma Nissé

Cover illustration and interior illustrations by Jane Smith

Photograph of Anna Del Conte by Katharine Davies

ISBN 978-1-912798-15-5

INTRODUCTION

Michelle says: It took me a long time to persuade Anna ro try combining classic Italian recipes with both gluten free and milk-free ingredients. Although she is still not always convinced by some of my milk/butter/cheese alternatives, she now has to agree that many of the gluten free alternatives, are really more than acceptable!!

Anna says: For a long time, Michelle kept asking me to write a book on gluten free Italian food, but I refused, because I didn't like the idea of having to exclude my beloved pasta from anything I wrote.

Then one day, Michelle sent me a large package. 'What is it?' I thought. I started unpacking, and out came bags and bags of different pasta: pasta made with rice flour, with cornflour, with beans... I was stunned, but I was even more stunned when I began to cook and eat it. 'Not bad,' I thought, 'not bad at all. Actually, some are very good.' Our collaboration is the result.

NATURALLY 'FREE-FROM'

A great deal of Italian food is naturally gluten and dairy-free, while, for those moving towards a plant-based lifestyle, Italian food is a treasure trove. Although a few of Anna's recipes in the book include fish or sausage, of the total, 92 per cent are vegetable or pulse based and totally meat and fish free. Yet, they are all classically Italian

COOKING WITH ANNA

For those of you who have never cooked with Anna before, do not be deceived by the simplicity of many of her recipes. I have lost track of how often I have said, 'Is that all?' – but then trusted her. The dish has been, invariably, delicious. For those of you who want to explore more of her recipes you will find all of her 20 plus books on Amazon and a good selection of them in most decent bookshops.

NOTES ON THE RECIPES AND INGREDIENTS

In this book, all the recipes are gluten free, most are milk-free and many and also meat-free. We have flagged them as the appropriate combination of:

Gluten free - GF

Milk-free - MF

Lactose-free - LF

Low lactose - LL

Gluten free pasta

You can now buy pasta made from a huge range of gluten free ingredients: corn, rice, quinoa, buckwheat, soya beans, chickpeas, black beans, low-calorie konjac and even seaweed – although strictly speaking you do not make seaweed pasta at all, you just harvest it.

Some of these – especially corn and rice-based pasta – come very close to the texture and flavour of a durum wheat pasta; although of course, they will never taste exactly the same because the base ingredients are different. For some of the dishes in the book (such as the fennel and anchovy sauce on page 25), that is what you need: a relatively mild, smooth pasta that will not overpower the delicate flavour of the sauce.

Others – the pulse-based pastas, for example – can be coarser in texture and stronger in flavour, but that does not at all invalidate them as a base for the sauce. It just means that you have to devise different sauces that suit them, which is exactly what Anna has done.

Some, such as the konjac or seaweed, bear very little resemblance to classic pasta at all – they have much chewier and chunkier textures – but still make an excellent and unusual base for the right sauce.

Pasta cooking times

We do not give cooking times for any of the gluten free pasta because, depending on what the pasta is made from, they could be very different. Therefore, please follow the instructions on each pack but also test regularly. We find that the times given are not always that accurate and can leave you with either under, or over or cooked pasta. Better to rely on your own tasting powers!

What is gluten free pasta made from?

Since pasta is essentially a mixture of flour and water you can, theoretically, make it out of any grain, legume or seed that can be ground into a relatively fine flour and then mixed with water.

However, in using a flour other wheat, you are hampered by:

How fine you can grind it? – it is hard, for example, to grind legumes as finely as grains, so chickpea and bean pasta tend to be coarser in texture than grain-based pasta.

How well it holds together – wheat-based pasta is helped by its gluten content but grains/legumes with lower levels of gluten or no gluten at all may tend to disintegrate.

The flavour – wheat, corn and rice are all mild in flavour but some of the grains (millet, quinoa, hemp) can be bitter. Some of the legumes can be quite strong. As a result, many of the alternative grains and seeds are only used in a blend with a milder ingredient such as rice or corn.

For all alternative pasta, follow the cooking instructions on the pack as they vary enormously – but do test it regularly during cooking to see if it is al dente, as the instructions are not always that reliable.

Bean, black and green – things have come on a lot in terms of bean pasta and the texture of most is now quite good although still somewhat coarser than a durum wheat pasta. Most do taste relatively 'beany', so need a strongly flavoured or spicy sauce. Made with lentils, soybeans or black beans, bean pasta has twice the protein, four times the fibre and fewer carbs than regular pasta.

Buckwheat – Buckwheat is not wheat; it is actually the seed of a flowering fruit that is related to rhubarb and sorrel. Buckwheat is usually combined with other gluten free flours as it tastes quite strong. It is dark in colour and its flavour is slightly nutty. Again, good with a vigorous sauce.

Chickpea/gram flour pasta – quite coarse in texture and yellow in colour. A slight legume flavour, but much enjoyed by many. Take care not to overcook it. Serve with a well flavoured or spicy sauce.

Corn/corn and rice – the most common of the alternative bases for pasta. Corn makes a smooth pasta, probably closest in texture to wheat-based pasta. Pure corn is quite yellow but is very mild, and slightly sweet in flavour. Be careful not to overcook it as it can be quite soft. It works well with relatively delicate sauces. When combined with rice, it has a slightly more neutral flavour and its yellowness is dimmed a bit.

Flaxseed and hemp seed pasta – both exist but are quite recherché so may not be easy to find. Nutritionally rich, they tend to be dark in both colour and flavour. They may also be combined with more neutral ingredients such as rice or corn. Flaxseed is a good source of fibre and Omega-3 fatty acid, while hemp seeds are rich in healthy fats and essential fatty acids. They also contain high amounts of vitamin E, calcium, iron, magnesium, phosphorus, potassium, sodium, sulphur and zinc.

Glass/cellophane noodles – a transparent noodle made from pure starch – usually mung bean, potato or tapioca. They are not really suitable for use as a traditional pasta but are good in soup, stir fries or spring rolls.

Konjac noodles – these are not made from grain at all but from the corm of a type of lily. They really do not have the texture of pasta at all but are valued because they have zero carbs and very few calories.

Millet seed – there are a few pure millet pastas, but it is more usual to find millet combined with rice or corn as on its own it is quite bitter. It is nutritionally rich, containing minerals like calcium, copper, iron, magnesium, phosphorus, potassium, and selenium as well as essential vitamins like folate, pantothenic acid, niacin, riboflavin, and vitamin B6, vitamin C, vitamin E, and vitamin K. Many of the most powerful health benefits millet has to offer are related to its high fibre content.

Quinoa – like flax, hemp and millet, quinoa is nutritionally rich, but on its own, can be slightly bitter. It is also expensive so is usually combined with rice and/or rice and corn. Quite pale in colour, it benefits from being combined with corn. Also high in fibre and rich in vitamins and minerals including, copper, folate, iron, phosphorus, manganese and zinc.

Rice/brown rice – White rice pasta is very pale in colour and mild in taste, so is usually combined with some other grain or flour. It is very soft so needs careful cooking. Good for very delicate sauces. Brown rice, which retains the husk of the rice grain, is much darker in colour and nuttier in both taste and texture. It keeps is texture well and works well with a variety of sauces. Not dissimilar in texture to a whole wheat pasta.

Soba noodles (buckwheat only) – buckwheat soba noodles are nutty and tasty but be careful, as although soba noodles are traditionally made from buckwheat, many commercial varieties these days a made with wheat.

Teff – comes from teff seeds which come from a grass native to the Horn of Africa. It is quite dark in colour, has a good texture and a slightly nutty flavour. It is also highly nutritious, rich in B vitamins and a great source of minerals including calcium, copper, iron, magnesium, manganese, phosphorus, potassium and zinc.

Milk-free and lactose-free

Confusingly, milk and lactose are not the same thing.

Milk-free

'Milk' on a food label refers to any milk-based food: milk itself, buttermilk, whey, cream, butter, yogurt, cheese, ice cream and any food which uses any of these. If you have a problem with milk-based foods, you can be:

Allergic – this means that you can have a potentially life-threatening immune system reaction to it.

Intolerant – which means that you may feel ill, sometimes seriously ill, but it will not be life-threatening. Whichever it is, you need to avoid all milk-based products.

Goat, sheep and buffalo milk

Although all animal milks share many characteristics, they are not identical, and there are some people who cannot tolerate cow's milk but can tolerate sheep, goat or buffalo milk. Although Parmigiano-Reggiano is made from cow's milk, pecorino (used in many of the recipes) is a sheep's milk cheese, so those people who are only sensitive to cow's milk may be okay with it.

Lactose and lactose intolerance

Lactose is the sugar found in all animal milk, including human. If you are lactose intolerant it means that you do not make enough of the enzyme lactase to process the lactose sugar in the milk. As a result, it ferments in your gut.

However, while there are relatively high levels of lactose sugar in straight milk, as the milk is processed into butter, yogurt or cheese, so the lactose sugar is broken down by the fermentation process.

The longer the cheese matures, the less lactose will remain. This means that really mature cheese such as Parmigiano-Reggiano or Pecorino Romano (the cheeses used almost exclusively in this book) will be suitable for someone on a low lactose diet.

Olive oil and extra virgin olive oil

Anna says: While I would always use extra virgin olive oil for dressing a salad, it is not necessary to do so for cooking although you certainly can if you prefer.

CONTENTS

Abbreviations: **GF** – gluten free, **MF** – milk-free, **LF** – lactose-free, **LL** – low lactose

SOUPS

Arugula/rocket and potato soup – **GF/can be MF/LL**

Broad bean soup – **GF/MF/LF**

Butternut squash and chicory soup – **GF/can be MF/LL**

Carrot soup – **GF/MF/LF**

Garlic soup – **GF/MF/LF**

Pea and pear soup – **GF/MF/LF**

Spinach and watercress soup – **GF/MF**

Zucchini/courgette soup – **GF/can be MF/LL**

ARUGULA/ROCKET AND POTATO SOUP

Gluten free/can be milk-free/low lactose

Anna: The grated cheese for this soup should be pecorino, which has the right pungency to match the rocket. If you cannot find Pecorino, use good, freshly grated Parmigiano-Reggiano.

Michelle: Using Pecorino or Parmigiano-Reggiano also means that this soup will be low lactose even though not, of course, milk-free. If you want to make it milk-free, leave off the cheese entirely (or use a vegan cheese) – it will still be very tasty.

SERVES 4

INGREDIENTS

4 oz/110g arugula/rocket leaves

handful of parsley leaves

1 small dried chilli, or more if you want it hotter

2–3 cloves garlic, according to size and how garlicy you want your soup

3 tbsp olive oil

8 oz/225g old potatoes

3 cups/24fl oz/750ml vegetable stock

sea salt and freshly ground black pepper

4 slices good quality, white, gluten free bread, toasted

2–3 tbsp freshly grated Pecorino or Parmigiano-Reggiano (optional)

METHOD

Wash and dry the arugula/rocket, remove any thick stalks and chop roughly.

Chop the parsley, chilli and garlic and put in a pot with 2 tablespoons of the oil. Sauté over a low heat – taking care that the garlic does not burn – until you start to smell the garlic aroma.

Peel and cut the potatoes into 1cm/½ inch cubes and add to the pot. Stir them around in the onion mixture until they are shiny and slightly translucent and then add the arugula/rocket. Stir and cook for 2–3 minutes.

Meanwhile, heat the stock. (Always heat any liquid before pouring it over potatoes as cold liquid will harden them.) Pour the stock over the potatoes, stir well and add a little salt. Turn the heat down and simmer for 40 minutes. Taste and check the seasoning.

Place a slice of toasted, gluten free bread in the bottom of each soup bowl and ladle the soup over it. Pour the rest of the oil directly into each bowl and hand the cheese around separately.

BROAD BEAN SOUP

Gluten free/milk-free/lactose-free

Anna: The broad beans from central Italy are the best in the world; they are so tiny and sweet that in Tuscany particularly, they are often eaten raw with local cheese, such as Pecorino. Broad beans taste much better when peeled, but I leave that to you! You can also make the soup with frozen broad beans.

Michelle: A lovely filling and naturally free-from soup. I do agree with Anna that the broad beans are much better peeled, especially as it is often hard to buy them when they are really young and tender.

SERVES 4

INGREDIENTS

3 lbs 8 oz/1.5kg fava beans/broad beans in their pods (or 12 oz/350g podded or frozen fava/broad beans, defrosted)

3 tbsp olive oil

1 large onion, cut into thin rings

1 garlic clove, sliced

1 lb 4 oz/500g ripe tomatoes, peeled and chopped

5 cups/2 pints/1.25 litres, gluten free vegetable stock

1 bay leaf

sea salt and freshly ground black pepper

a dozen leaves of fresh mint, roughly chopped

METHOD

If you are using fresh beans, remove them from their pods. If you are going to peel them, cook them for 1–2 minutes in boiling water, then remove them and plunge into cold water. After a couple of minutes, you will be able to break the skin on the end of the bean with a knife or your nail, and pop out the lovely green beans inside. Set them aside.

Heat the oil in a saucepan, add the onion and sauté until golden. Add the garlic, fry for a minute and then throw in the beans and fry for 30 seconds, stirring all the time.

Add the tomatoes and fry for a further 10 minutes, stirring frequently. Keep an eye on the pot and add a little stock if the tomatoes are getting burnt.

Pour in all the stock, add the bay leaf, cover and cook for about 7–8 minutes until the beans are tender. Taste and add salt and pepper and remove the bay leaf.

Ladle the soup into individual bowls and sprinkle over the mint leaves. Serve at once.

BUTTERNUT SQUASH AND ENDIVE/CHICORY SOUP

Gluten free/can be milk-free/low lactose

Anna says: This recipe comes from Mantua, a province in the Lombardy region of northern Italy, where it would be made with pumpkin rather than butternut squash as the Mantovans pride themselves on their pumpkins. However, I am afraid that I think it actually works better with butternut squash, which is also easier to find.

Michelle says: The original recipe used butter, but olive oil works just as well, and the soup already has loads of flavour, without the Parmigiano-Reggiano garnish, if you want to make it milk-free. And if you are just avoiding lactose, then you will be good with the Parmigiano-Reggiano anyhow.

SERVES 4

INGREDIENTS

9 oz/250g peeled butternut squash

1 good-sized head endive/chicory

6 tbsp olive oil

1 small onion, peeled and chopped

5 cups/2 pints/1.25 litres gluten free vegetable stock

sea salt and freshly ground black pepper

2 slices gluten free, firm-textured white bread, crusts removed

freshly grated Parmigiano-Reggiano (optional)

METHOD

Cut the squash into cubes and slice the endive/chicory thickly. Wash the endive/chicory and drain.

Heat 3 tablespoons of the oil in a large pan and add the onion and a pinch of salt to stop it burning. Gently sauté for 7–8 minutes then add the squash. Continue to cook for another five minutes, turning the cubes frequently, then add the chicory and continue to cook for a few more minutes.

Heat 4 cups/1 ¾ pints /1 litre of the stock and pour it over the vegetables. Mix well and season with salt and pepper. Cover, bring to the boil and simmer for 30 minutes or until the squash is tender.

While the soup is cooking make the crostini by first heating the oven to 400°F/190°C/Gas Mark 6. Cut the bread into 1 inch/3cm cubes. Pour the remaining oil into a bowl and mix the bread cubes well in the oil. Spread them in a single layer onto a baking sheet. Bake for 10 minutes, shaking the tray once or twice during that time.

When the squash is cooked, purée the soup with a stick blender or in a liquidiser or food processor and adjust the seasoning to taste. If you want the soup thinner, add a little extra stock.

Ladle the soup into individual bowls and drop a handful of the crostini into each bowl.

CARROT SOUP

Gluten free/milk-free/lactose-free

Anna says: This is a smooth soup, excellent served either hot or cold. It is also quick and easy to make.

Michelle says: And totally free-from...

SERVES 4

INGREDIENTS

4 tbsp olive oil

2 shallots, peeled and chopped

1 lb 2 oz/500g carrots
cut into thick discs

2 oz/50g piece fresh ginger, peeled

5 cups/2 pints/1.25 litre
gluten free vegetable stock

sea salt and freshly ground black pepper

METHOD

Heat the oil in a pan and add the shallot, and 2 pinches of salt, and sauté gently over a very low heat stirring continually until the shallots soften and become golden.

Add the carrots and grate in the ginger. Mix again and cook for 5–6 minutes, turning the carrots over and over. Add the stock, bring to the boil and simmer gently for 25 minutes or until the carrots are soft.

Purée the soup with a stick blender or in a liquidiser or food processor – the latter will give a smoother soup. Taste, and adjust the seasoning before serving.

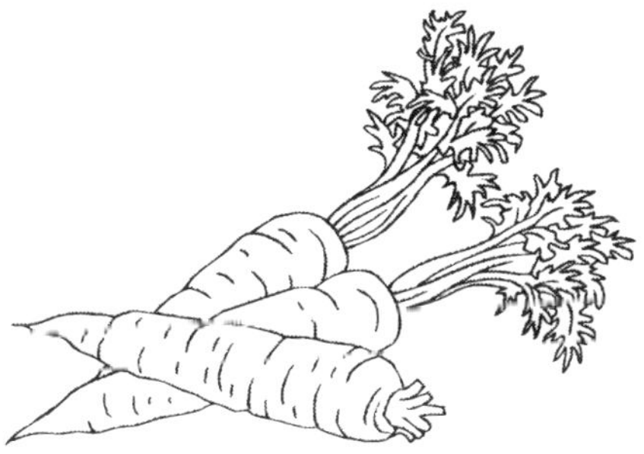

GARLIC SOUP

Gluten free/milk-free/lactose-free

Anna: The origin of this soup is half-French and half-Portuguese. The result is Italian, but it could be from anywhere where garlic is used and loved. It seems to contain an awful lot of garlic, but because it is properly cooked, the result is quite delicate.

Michelle: This is a delicious soup if you like garlic, so I was keen to find a milk-free way to make it. Using 3 tablespoons of a mild olive oil instead of the butter and 4 tablespoons of milk-free plain soya or coconut yogurt instead of the soured cream, seemed to work pretty well.

SERVES 4

INGREDIENTS

2 large red onions, chopped

2 sprigs thyme

3 tbsp olive oil

sea salt

1 small garlic bulb, peeled and chopped roughly

2 large potatoes, cut into small cubes

2 bay leaves

3½ cups/1½ pints/900ml hot, gluten free vegetable stock

3 tbsp milk-free plain soya or coconut yoghurt

a pinch of grated nutmeg

small bunch of chives, chopped

METHOD

Gently fry the onion and thyme in oil without burning. Add a pinch of salt. Cover with a lid and continue to fry gently, stirring frequently, until the onion is soft.

Add all the garlic and continue to cook slowly for 10 minutes, stirring frequently. Add the potatoes and the bay leaves and cook for 5 minutes. Gradually mix in the hot vegetable stock while stirring constantly. Simmer, covered, until the potatoes are done – it should take about 10 minutes.

Discard the bay leaves and purée the soup with a stick blender or in a liquidiser or food processor; if it is too thick, add a little stock. Mix in the yoghurt and nutmeg.

Taste. Adjust the seasoning and ladle the soup into individual bowls. Sprinkle on the chives and serve.

PEA AND PEAR SOUP

Gluten free/milk-free/lactose-free

Anna says: This is not a classic Italian recipe although it was given to me by an Italian. Whatever its origins, it is well worth making!

Michelle says: The original recipe used butter and garnished the soup with a swirl of cream. However, olive oil works just as well, and I personally think, that the cream somewhat masks the flavour of the soup!

SERVES 4

INGREDIENTS

1 onion, very finely sliced

4 tbsp olive oil

sea salt

12 mint leaves, torn

2 ripe pears, peeled and cut into small pieces

1 lb 2 oz/500g frozen peas

4 cups/1¾ pints/1 litre gluten free vegetable stock

freshly ground black pepper

METHOD

Gently sauté the onion, together with a pinch of salt and half the torn mint leaves in the oil for 8–10 minutes, stirring frequently. The onion should become soft and golden brown.

Add the pear to the onion. Sauté for 1 minute and then add the frozen peas with all their ice attached. Mix well and then add the stock. Bring to the boil and simmer for 25 minutes.

Blend the soup with a stick blender or in a liquidiser or food processor and season to taste. Sprinkle a little mint over each bowlful before serving.

SPINACH AND WATERCRESS SOUP

Gluten free/milk-free

Anna says: This is not a traditional Italian recipe but is nonetheless a favourite of mine. I particularly like it because the watercress is not really cooked but just heated through, so it keeps its distinctive peppery flavour.

Michelle says: The original of this soup had some cream swirled into it before it was served but I do not think the cream added anything to the flavour of the soup – if anything, it masked it! However, Anna's suggestion of a few chilli flakes definitely does add something.

SERVES 4

INGREDIENTS

4 tbsp olive oil

1 large onion, chopped

1 x 14 oz/400g can of cannellini beans

4 cups/1½ pints/1 litre gluten free vegetable stock

1 bunch watercress, washed, stalks discarded

9 oz/250g frozen spinach, unthawed

salt and freshly ground black pepper

crushed chilli flakes

METHOD

Heat the oil in a large pan and add the onion together with a pinch of salt. Gently sauté the onion for a few minutes, stirring frequently so that it becomes soft and slightly coloured but not golden. Add the frozen spinach and allow it to defrost in the pan.

Drain and rinse the cannellini beans and add to the soup along with the stock. Simmer all together for 5–8 minutes to allow the beans to absorb the flavour of the spinach.

Add the watercress to the saucepan and mix well then remove from the heat. The watercress should wilt, not cook.

Purée with a stick blender or in a liquidiser or food processor. Season to taste and serve sprinkled with a few chilli flakes in each bowl.

ZUCCHINI/COURGETTE SOUP

Gluten free/can be milk-free/low lactose

Anna says: This soup is a soft, pale green colour and is as attractive as it is delicious. The eggs added at the end of the cooking should curdle and thicken the broth.

Michelle says: Although the classic version of this soup should be creamy, it actually is still lovely if you just leave out the cream and the Parmigiano-Reggiano and use an extra tablespoon of oil for cooking the courgette. Indeed, some would say that the flavour of the courgettes comes through even better, as it is not masked by the cream and the cheese!

SERVES 4

INGREDIENTS

12 oz/350g zucchini/courgettes, cut into short matchsticks

1 banana shallot, peeled and chopped

3 tbsp olive oil

4½ cups/2 pints/1.1 litres gluten free vegetable stock

2 egg yolks

3 tbsp Parmigiano-Reggiano, grated (optional)

a pinch or two of grated nutmeg

sea salt and freshly ground black pepper

METHOD

Place the zucchini/courgettes in a colander, sprinkle with salt and leave to drain for 20–30 minutes. Dry them thoroughly with absorbent kitchen paper.

Put the shallot with the oil in a saucepan and cook gently until the shallot is translucent – but do not let it get brown or turn golden. Add the zucchini/courgette and sauté for 2–3 minutes, stirring all the time.

Pour in the stock, cover the pan and simmer for 15 minutes.

Gently beat together the egg yolks, cheese, (if you are using it) nutmeg and seasoning. Pour the mixture into the soup, stirring well. Boil for 1 minute, then serve at once.

SPQR

PASTA

Chickpea or buckwheat pasta with garlic, oil and rosemary – **GF/MF/LF**

Bean or buckwheat pasta with broccoli sauce – **GF/can be MF/LL**

Any gluten free pasta with leek sauce – **GF/can be MF**

Black bean spaghetti with mussel sauce – **GF/MF/LF**

Gluten free pasta with fennel sauce – **GF/can be MF/LL**

Smoked salmon and pesto sauce for any gluten free pasta – **GF/MF/LF**

Gluten free pasta with tomato and anchovy sauce – **GF/MF/LF**

Mushrooms and anchovy pasta bake – **GF/can be MF/LL**

CHICKPEA OR BUCKWHEAT PASTA WITH GARLIC, OLIVE OIL AND ROSEMARY

Gluten free/milk-free/lactose-free

Anna says: This is a robust, piquant sauce ideal for chickpea or buckwheat pasta. You might like to put in more chilli pepper or less. Taste it – careful, a tiny bit is quite enough – and decide for yourself.

Michelle says: A great, simple and totally free-from dish.

SERVES 4

INGREDIENTS

14 oz/400g chickpea or buckwheat fusilli or penne

7 tbsp olive oil

4 garlic cloves, finely chopped

1–2 fresh chilli peppers, cores and seeds removed, finely chopped

2 rosemary sprigs, finely chopped

2 tsp lemon juice

METHOD

Cook the pasta in plenty of well salted, boiling water according to the instructions on the pack.

While the pasta is cooking, heat the olive oil in a large frying pan. When hot, throw in the chopped garlic, chilli and rosemary and fry, stirring constantly for 1 minute, pressing the ingredients to release the juices.

Drain the pasta and turn it immediately into the frying pan. Now stir it over and over so that all the shapes can get thoroughly dressed.

Sprinkle with the lemon juice, stir again and serve at once, straight from the pan.

BEAN OR BUCKWHEAT PASTA WITH BROCCOLI SAUCE

Gluten free/can be milk-free/low lactose

Anna says: Broccoli sauce is a classic of southern Italian cooking and it is one of the best for chickpea pasta, although you certainly could use it successfully with any other gluten free pasta.

Michelle says: This sauce is naturally gluten and milk-free apart from the Pecorino Romano, which is optional anyhow. However, Pecorino is made from sheep's milk, not cow's milk, so if you are only intolerant of cow's milk, you may be able to eat it. It is also a long-matured cheese, which means that it will be very low lactose if you are lactose, not milk, intolerant.

SERVES 4

INGREDIENTS

1 lb 2 oz/500g broccoli florets

14 oz/400g gluten free pasta (orecchiette would be excellent but if not, penne is also good)

6 tbsp olive oil

3 garlic cloves, chopped

6 anchovy fillets, drained and chopped

1 dried chilli, seeded and chopped

4 tbsp freshly grated Pecorino Romano (optional)

METHOD

Cut the broccoli into small florets. Remove the outer layer of the stalks and cut the stalks into small pieces. Wash and plunge them into a pan of rapidly boiling well salted water. Cook until just tender, then lift them out of the water with a slotted spoon and put in a colander to drain; retain the cooking water to cook the pasta.

Cook the pasta in the broccoli stock, according to the instructions on the pack. If there is not enough stock to cook the pasta – you will need at least 3.5 litres of liquid – add boiling water and more salt.

Meanwhile, heat the olive oil in a large frying pan. Throw in the garlic, anchovies and chilli, and sauté for a minute or two, while pounding the ingredients down to release their flavour. Add the broccoli and fry gently for some 5 minutes, stirring frequently.

When cooked, drain the pasta and turn it immediately into the broccoli sauce. Stir on the heat for a good 2 minutes and serve with a bowl of Pecorino Romano on the side, if you are using it.

MUSHROOM AND ANCHOVY PASTA BAKE

Gluten free/can be milk-free/low lactose

Anna says: This is one of the most successful pasta bakes that we've made – easy to prepare, and even easier to eat!

Michelle says: And totally free-from!

SERVES 4

INGREDIENTS

½ oz/15g dried porcini mushrooms

12 oz/350g brown mushrooms

8 tbsp olive oil (with extra oil for greasing the dish)

2 garlic cloves, chopped

2 anchovy fillets, drained

rind of 1 unwaxed lemon and juice of ½ lemon

sea salt and freshly ground black pepper

2 oz/50g dried gluten free breadcrumbs

2 tbsp flat-leaf parsley, chopped

a pinch or two of chilli flakes

14 oz/400g any gluten free penne or fusilli

1 tbsp gluten free basil pesto – or gluten and milk-free basil pesto for a milk-free version

METHOD

Preheat the oven to 350°F/180°C/Gas Mark 4.

Soak the porcini in a bowl of hot water for 20 minutes. When the time is up, drain the porcini, keeping the liquid, and chop them coarsely.

While the porcini soak, clean the mushrooms and slice them (if they are large, cut them in half and then slice). Heat 4 tablespoons of the olive oil in a large frying pan, add the garlic and anchovies and sauté gently, pounding the mixture in the bottom of the pan.

Now throw in the brown mushrooms and fry them over a lively heat, while turning them to make sure they get coated in the oil. After 5 minutes, add the drained porcini and continue to fry for a further 5 minutes.

Add the lemon juice, salt and pepper and turn the heat down. Cook gently for about 10 minutes, adding some more of the porcini liquid whenever the sauce gets too dry.

Heat the remaining oil in a clean frying pan and, when hot, throw in the gluten free breadcrumbs and lemon rind. Fry for 2 minutes, or until the crumbs are golden, stirring the whole time. Then add the parsley and chilli and continue to fry for 30 seconds.

Meanwhile, cook the pasta in plenty of well salted boiling water according to the instructions on the pack. Drain and tip it immediately into the mushroom sauce, then add the pesto. Stir constantly over a gentle heat for a minute or two.

Oil a large shallow oven dish and sprinkle with gluten free breadcrumbs. Tip in the pasta, spread it out to cover the bottom of the dish, then spoon the fried breadcrumb mixture over the top.

Bake for 15 minutes. Allow to rest for a couple of minutes before serving.

SMOKED SALMON AND PESTO SAUCE FOR ANY GLUTEN FREE PASTA

Gluten free/milk-free/lactose-free

Anna says: My Italian daughter-in-law gave me this delicious sauce when I was staying with her and my son. Smoked salmon is one of the few foreign foods that are now part of the Italian food scene: it is eaten usually with green salad, but it is also combined with Italian ingredients, as in this sauce. You can be more adventurous and use either a vegetable spiralizer or – our preference – seaweed spaghetti or tagliatelle. These will have a chewier texture than any pasta but are rather delicious and certainly unusual.

Michelle says: Simple and delicious. I love the idea of using seaweed: not only super-healthy, but absolutely on trend – just where free-from ought to be!

SERVES 4

INGREDIENTS

14 oz/400g brown rice spaghetti, or approximately 80g seaweed spaghetti or tagliatelle
NB: Seaweed pasta swells up to five times its size when cooked.

8 tbsp gluten free basil pesto – or gluten and milk-free basil pesto for the milk-free version

10 oz/300g smoked salmon

4 tbsp extra virgin olive oil

sea salt and freshly ground black pepper

METHOD

Cook the pasta in plenty of well salted boiling water according to the instructions on the pack. If you are using the seaweed pasta, you will need to boil it for 10–15 minutes. It will never get as soft as pasta but should be just pleasantly *al dente*.

While the pasta is cooking, put the pesto in a large, heatproof serving bowl and place the bowl in a warm oven at 200°F/ 90°C/Gas ¼. Next, cut the salmon into short strips.

When the pasta is cooked, drain, reserving a mugful of the cooking water, and turn it into the warm bowl. Add the olive oil, half of the salmon and enough of the pasta water to loosen the sauce.

Season with a good grind of black pepper, taste and add salt if necessary. Mix well using two forks to lift the strands up in the air, scatter the remaining salmon over the top, and serve.

ANY GLUTEN FREE PASTA WITH LEEK SAUCE

Gluten free/can be milk-free

Anna says: Leeks are quite popular in Northern Italy but are not often made into a pasta sauce. However, because I like them very much, I created this sauce in which I have used turmeric – very non-Italian! I used this with a rice and maize flour fusilli.

Michelle says: Anna maintains that the flavour of the butter is crucial to this dish, so she was reluctant to allow me to suggest using olive oil, or even a milk-free spread or coconut oil. However, if you want to make the sauce milk/dairy-free, just use 2 oz/50g of a dairy-free spread or coconut oil instead of the butter – but remember that it will not taste quite as Anna intended (although you might like it even more!) Remember that if you are lactose, rather than milk, intolerant, you may be able to eat the Parmigiano-Reggiano.

SERVES 4

INGREDIENTS

1lb 2 oz/500g leeks, white part only (NB: this is the weight of the leeks needed for the sauce, not the whole leeks)

2 oz/50g unsalted butter or dairy-free spread/coconut oil for the milk-free version

4 tbsp olive oil

sea salt and freshly ground black pepper

⅔ cup/5fl oz/150ml gluten free vegetable stock

¾ tsp turmeric

14 oz/400g rice and maize fusilli

grated Parmigiano-Reggiano (optional)

METHOD

Preheat the oven to 200°F/90°C/Gas ¼).

Cut the leeks into very thin rounds, put them in a sink of water and wash very well. Scoop the leeks up and place in a colander to drain.

Heat 1 oz/25g of the butter, spread or coconut oil and all of the olive oil, in a large sauté pan. When the butter foam begins to subside, add the leeks a little at a time, so that you can coat them in the fat more easily.

When all the leeks are in the pan, add a generous pinch of salt and cook over a lively heat for 2–3 minutes, while you stir the whole time. Pour in about half the stock, mix well and cover the pan with a lid.

Cook for some 30 minutes, turning the leeks over occasionally and adding a little more stock if necessary. After 15 minutes, season with the turmeric and plenty of pepper, mix thoroughly and continue cooking until the leeks are totally mashed – a liquid sauce of a lovely yellowy-green colour. Taste and adjust the seasoning.

Meanwhile, cook the pasta in plenty of well salted boiling water according to the instructions on the pack. While the pasta is cooking, put the remaining 1oz/25g butter, spread or coconut oil, in a heatproof serving bowl and place the bowl in the oven.

When the pasta is ready, drain and turn it immediately into the warmed bowl, mix thoroughly with the butter or spread, spoon over the sauce and serve with a bowl of Parmigiano-Reggiano on the side if you are using it.

GLUTEN FREE PASTA WITH TOMATO AND ANCHOVY SAUCE

Gluten free/milk-free/lactose-free

Anna says: Most gluten free pastas have a stronger flavour than wheat-based pastas, so they need good, strongly flavoured sauces such as this.

Michelle says: Agreed!

SERVES 4

INGREDIENTS

6 tbsp olive oil

4 garlic cloves, peeled and sliced

8 anchovy fillets, drained and chopped

½ tsp chilli flakes (more if you want it really hot)

sea salt

1 x 14 oz/400g and 1 x 7 oz/225g tins chopped plum tomatoes

14 oz/400g gluten free spaghetti (brown rice spaghetti would work well)

1 tsp dried oregano

2 tbsp capers

METHOD

Heat 4 tablespoons of the olive oil in a large frying pan and, when hot, throw in the garlic and anchovies. Sauté gently for about 2 minutes, squashing the anchovies down against the bottom of the pan to release the flavour.

Add the chilli, salt and tinned tomatoes. Turn the heat up and cook for 10 minutes, or until the sauced has thickened, stirring frequently. Taste and adjust the salt and chilli to your liking.

Meanwhile, cook the pasta in plenty of well salted boiling water according to the instructions on the pack. When cooked, drain the pasta, reserving a mugful of the cooking water. Tip the pasta straight into the frying pan with the sauce.

Stir on the heat for approximately 2 minutes, adding some of the reserved cooking water if necessary (some gluten free pasta needs more liquid than others). Pour over the remaining 2 tablespoons of olive oil. Sprinkle over the oregano and capers and serve at once.

GLUTEN FREE PASTA WITH FENNEL SAUCE

Gluten free/milk-free/lactose-free

Anna says: A delicious sauce with any pasta – we are sure you will love it.

Michelle says: Too right – and naturally free-from!

SERVES 4

INGREDIENTS

1–2 fennel bulbs, about 1lb/450g

½ cup/4fl oz/120ml olive oil

6 anchovy fillets, drained and chopped

2 garlic cloves, chopped

sea salt and freshly ground black pepper

1 tbsp fennel seeds

14 oz/400g any rice or corn-based penne or fusilli

12 plain black olives, pitted

METHOD

Cut the feathery fronds off the stalks of the fennel and reserve. Cut the stalks off the bulbs then throw them away. Cut the bulb into quarters lengthwise, and then into thin strips. Wash under cold water and then leave in a colander to drain.

Take a large sauté pan with a lid and pour in about half of the olive oil. Add the anchovies and garlic and sauté for a minute or two, while pressing the mixture down with a fork against the bottom of the pan to release the juices. Remove as much of the anchovy and garlic from the oil as you can and set aside.

Throw the fennel into the pan, a little at a time, so that all the pieces of fennel can absorb some of the garlicky oil. When all the fennel is in the pan, cook over a lively heat for some 5 minutes, turning the fennel over and over.

Add a generous pinch of salt and 2 tablespoons of hot water. Turn down the heat and cover the pan. Cook very slowly until the fennel is very tender, so tender that you can mush it up with a fork – it will take at least half an hour to cook. Keep an eye on the sauce during the cooking; you will have to add a few extra tablespoons of hot water 2 or 3 times during the cooking. The fennel should be cooking all the time in quite a bit of liquid.

While the fennel is cooking, put the fennel seeds in a mortar and pound them with a pestle until broken up. Add to the fennel sauce together with a generous grind of pepper. Mix well, taste and adjust the salt.

Meanwhile, cook the pasta in plenty of well salted boiling water according to the instructions on the pack.

Drain the pasta, reserving a cupful of the cooking water. Tip the pasta into the fennel sauce. Add the reserved chopped garlic and anchovies and the remaining olive oil and mix very well, adding some of the pasta water to loosen the sauce.

Spoon the pasta into a warmed bowl and keep it warm while you chop the reserved fennel tops. Sprinkle these over the top of the pasta, throw in the black olives and serve.

BLACK BEAN SPAGHETTI WITH MUSSEL SAUCE

Gluten free/can be milk-free/can be low lactose

Anna says: We used this sauce to dress black bean spaghetti and decided it was perfect but it is such a good sauce, we are sure it would work well with any other gluten free pasta.

Michelle says: Pulse-based pastas are now becoming quite common. They tend to have a rather different, coarser texture than wheat, corn, or rice-based pasta, and a fairly vigorous flavour so are best matched with strong-flavoured sauces such as this. If pushed for time, you could use frozen mussels – although the flavour will not be quite as good, it will still be pretty spectacular. Any standard basil pesto should be gluten free but if you want to make the dish milk/dairy-free as well, Saclà make an excellent milk-free basil pesto and I am sure there are others.

SERVES 4

INGREDIENTS

400g black bean spaghetti

2lbs 8 oz/1kg fresh mussels in their shells, or 1 lb 2 oz/500g frozen mussels

IF YOU ARE USING FRESH MUSSELS:
1 lemon, cut in half

3 garlic cloves, peeled and squashed

3 tbsp olive oil

FOR THE SAUCE:
1 tbsp olive oil

1 clove garlic, peeled and crushed

½ tsp flaked chilli
(or more, according to taste)

3 tbsp flat-leaf parsley, chopped

1 tbsp gluten free basil pesto – or gluten and milk-free basil pesto for the milk-free version

$\frac{2}{3}$ cup/5fl oz/150ml white wine

a squeeze or two of lemon juice

sea salt

METHOD

First prepare the fresh mussels or defrost the frozen mussels, reserving their juices.

For the fresh mussels:
Mussels these days are usually sold already clean; if not, wash them in a sink of cold water, scrubbing them hard, removing barnacles and beard. Remove and throw away any mussel which remains open when you tap it on a hard surface – that means that it is dead. Put the lemon halves, 3 garlic cloves and 3 tablespoons of olive oil in a large sauté pan with a tight-fitting lid, add the mussels and put the lid on the pan.

Put the pan on a high heat and cook for 4–5 minutes, shaking it occasionally to allow all the mussels to get in touch with the bottom of the pan. All the mussels should be open by now. As soon as they are cool enough to touch, remove the flesh from the shells, letting the lovely juices fall back into the pan.

Put the mussels in a bowl and discard the shells and the lemon. Have a look at the juices. If there is some grit at the bottom of the pan, strain the juices through a fine sieve. Nowadays mussels are mostly farmed, so not very dirty; this step is not often necessary. Set the mussels aside and keep warm while you cook the pasta and make the sauce.

Cook the pasta in plenty of well salted boiling water according to the instructions on the pack.

To make the sauce:

While the pasta is cooking, put a sauté pan on the heat with 1 tablespoon olive oil. Heat it and add the garlic, chilli and 2 tablespoons of the parsley. Fry for 1 minute and as soon as the garlic aroma rises, add the pesto, mussel juices and wine. Boil briskly for a couple of minutes to reduce the juices by approximately one-third.

If you are using frozen mussels, turn them into the pan and continue to cook gently for a couple of minutes to heat the mussels through in the sauce without letting them break up. If you are using fresh, add them to the sauce just before serving and make sure they are well coated.

When the pasta is ready, drain and turn it into a warmed serving bowl. Spoon the mussels and sauce over the top, sprinkle with the remaining tablespoon of parsley and squeeze over the lemon juice. Serve immediately.

THERESIANER
CONTRA
S.FAUSTINO
152
SPINGERE

RICE DISHES

Arancini – **GF/can be MF/LL**

Risotto with Jerusalem artichokes – **GF**

Risotto with asparagus – **GF/can be MF/can be LL**

Risotto with spinach – **GF/MF/LF**

Bean and vegetable risotto soup – **GF/MF/LF**

Mushroom risotto – **GF/can be MF/can be LL**

Oven-baked risotto – **GF/can be MF/LL**

Rice with peas – **GF/can be MF/LL**

Risotto with prawns and peas – **GF/can be MF**

Tomatoes stuffed with rice and potatoes – **GF/MF/LF**

Rice and zucchini/courgette or leek torta – **GF/LL**

ARANCINI

Gluten free/can be milk-free/low lactose

Anna says: Arancini are an excellent way of using up left over risotto but if you do not have any leftovers you can very well make them from scratch. It makes them much more fun if you bury a pea, or a piece of mozzarella, or if you eat meat, a piece of salami or sausage in the middle of each ball.

Michelle says: Anna's recipe for arancini includes Pecorino and Parmigiano-Reggiano, both of which are very low lactose but not of course, milk-free. If you wanted to make the arancini milk-free you could substitute olive oil for the butter and chillies, or pine nuts for the cheese, as below.

MAKES 12 ARANCINI

INGREDIENTS

6 oz/170g risotto rice

gluten free vegetable stock

2 free range eggs

2 tbsp soft, unsalted butter, or extra virgin olive oil

1 oz/25g Pecorino or Parmigiano-Reggiano or a mixture of the two, finely grated – or for the milk-free version – ½ tsp chilli or paprika powder or 1oz/25g pine nuts, roughly chopped

sea salt and freshly ground black pepper

handful of frozen petits pois

2 tbsp plain gluten free flour

2 oz/50g plain gluten free breadcrumbs

olive oil to fry the arancini

METHOD

If you do not have any leftover risotto, cook the rice in plenty of boiling gluten free vegetable stock for approximately 12 minutes or until the rice is soft but not mushy.

Drain, reserving the stock for soup, and tip the rice into a bowl. Allow the rice to cool a bit.

Add 1 egg, the butter or olive oil, the cheese or the chilli/paprika/pine nuts, to the rice. Mix thoroughly and then season to taste with sea salt and freshly ground black pepper.

Chill the rice mixture thoroughly.

When ready to cook, with damp hands pick up small handfuls of rice and shape them into balls about the size of a golf ball. Push a couple of peas (or mozzarella, salami or sausage) into the middle or each ball.

Spread some gluten free flower on a plate and roll each ball in flour.

Beat the remaining egg on a plate and spread the breadcrumbs on another plate. Heat the oil in a flattish pan. Roll each ball in the egg, let any excess drip off, then roll it in the breadcrumbs.

Fry gently in the oil, taking care not to burn the balls, until they are golden brown and crisp. They are good straight from the pan or at room temperature.

RISOTTO WITH JERUSALEM ARTICHOKES

Gluten free

Anna says: I don't peel Jerusalem artichokes (too difficult); I scrub them vigorously with a hard brush under running water. Saclà truffle pesto, which is quite delicious, is a perfect complement to Jerusalem artichokes.

Michelle says: This is one of the few recipes in this book where I have given in to Anna and agreed that the butter, truffle pesto and Parmigiano-Reggiano are so crucial to the dish that it would be difficult to create a milk-free version that would actually work. So, for gluten free diners only I'm afraid!

SERVES 4

INGREDIENTS

14 oz/400g Jerusalem artichokes, trimmed of their more protuberant nobbles

6 cups/2½ pints/1.5 litres hot, gluten free vegetable stock

2 oz/50g unsalted butter

2 tbsp olive oil

2 tbsp onion, chopped

sea salt

14 oz/400g Italian rice (e.g. Arborio, Carnaroli, Vialone Nano)

4 tbsp dry sherry, such as Manzanilla

2 tsp Saclà truffle pesto (contains milk, cashew nuts and egg)

2 oz/50g Parmigiano Reggiano, grated

freshly ground black pepper

METHOD

Wash and scrub the Jerusalem artichokes and cut them into small cubes. Heat the stock and keep it at nearly boiling point all the time while you make the risotto.

Heat half the butter and all of the olive oil in your risotto pan – a deep sauté pan is perfect. Throw in the onion, sprinkle with a pinch of salt and sauté for a good 7–8 minutes until it is soft and golden, but not brown.

Add the Jerusalem artichokes and continue frying gently for 5 minutes, stirring the vegetable dice around with the onion. Now add the rice, mix with the vegetables and sauté for 2–3 minutes until the grains are translucent and well coated with butter and olive oil. Pour in the sherry and boil briskly to evaporate.

Add the stock one ladleful at a time. Mix well and continuing to cook until that ladleful has been absorbed, then add another – and then another until the rice is cooked. (Good Italian rice cooks in about 18–20 minutes, depending on the variety). You might not need all the stock; on the other hand, if you have no more stock left, just add boiling water. When the rice is al dente – or cooked as you like it – mix in the Saclà truffle pesto and remove the pan from the heat.

Add the remaining butter and cheese. Turn the heat off. Put the lid on the pan and let the risotto rest for 2 minutes before you give it a final energetic stir. Grind over some black pepper and bring it to the table.

RISOTTO WITH ASPARAGUS

Gluten free/can be milk-free/can be low lactose

Anna says: This is one of the most deliciously delicate risotti I know. Some cooks add 2 tablespoons of cream at the end of the cooking, but I prefer to stick to the traditional butter.

Michelle says: Anna says that risotto should always be cooked with butter rather than oil, as the rice does not absorb the oil. The butter will also give a very specific and delicate flavour to the dish. However, if you cannot eat butter, it seems a shame to deprive you of this really delicious dish so... To make the dish totally milk-free, substitute 3 tablespoons of a light olive oil for the butter and leave out the Parmigiano-Reggiano. Or if you are just avoiding lactose, use olive oil, but you may be able to use the Parmigiano-Reggiano.

SERVES 4

INGREDIENTS

12 oz/350g asparagus

8 cups/3 pints/2 litres gluten free vegetable stock

3 oz/75g unsalted butter or 3 tbsp light olive oil

2 shallots, finely chopped

12 oz/350g Italian rice (e.g. Arborio, Carnaroli, Vialone Nano)

2 tbsp white vermouth

sea salt and freshly ground black pepper

4 oz/110g freshly grated Parmigiano Reggiano (optional)

METHOD

Wash and trim the asparagus, cut off the hard ends of the stalks, and put in a saucepan with the stock and bring to the boil. Boil for 15 minutes. (NB: you are cooking the hard stalks in the stock to give it flavour; you will not be using them in the dish.) Scoop out and discard the stalks, and keep the stock nearly boiling for the whole cooking time, since you must add simmering liquid to the rice.

Cut the tender part of the asparagus into roughly ¾ inch/2 cm pieces and set aside the spear tops. Heat half the butter or oil, add the shallots and sauté gently until soft. Add the asparagus pieces, but not the spears. Sauté gently for 5 minutes, stirring constantly, then add the rice.

Continue cooking until the grains appear translucent and well coated with the butter or oil. Splash with the vermouth, cook for a minute or two, then begin to add the stock one ladleful at a time. When the rice looks dry, add another ladleful and then another ladleful, until the rice is cooked. If you have finished all the stock and the rice is not cooked to your liking, simply add extra boiling water.

About 5 minutes, before the rice is ready, (good Italian rice takes about 18–20 minutes to cook, depending on the variety) add the top spears and salt and pepper to taste. When the rice is done, turn off the heat, add the remaining butter or oil and half the Parmigiano Reggiano if you are using it. Cover the pan and leave the risotto to rest for 2 minutes.

Stir energetically and bring to the table with a bowl of the remaining Parmigiano Reggiano – if you are using it – on the side.

RISOTTO WITH SPINACH

Gluten free/milk-free/lactose-free

Anna says: You can make this risotto milk-free by simply replacing the butter with 6 tablespoons of olive oil. It is just as delicious, although with a slightly different flavour.

Michelle says: Yes, it is!

SERVES 4

INGREDIENTS

5 cups/2 pints/1.25 litres gluten free vegetable stock

1 lb/450g cooked spinach (or frozen spinach leaf, defrosted)

either 3 oz/80g unsalted butter and 1 tbsp olive oil or 6 tbsp olive oil

1 small onion, chopped

12 oz/350g Italian rice (e.g. Arborio, Carnaroli, Vialone Nano)

2/3 cup/5fl oz/150ml dry white wine

6 canned anchovy fillets, drained

1 garlic clove

sea salt and freshly ground black pepper

METHOD

Heat the stock and keep it just simmering for the whole time that you cook the rice.

Using your hands, squeeze any liquid out of the spinach and chop it roughly.

Heat the butter and olive oil (or just the oil) in your risotto pan. When the butter is turning a hazelnut colour, throw in the onion and sauté for 5–6 minutes. Add the spinach and continue to sauté for a few more minutes, turning the whole mixture over and over.

Now add the rice and fry it over a lively heat until all the grains become translucent. Splash with the wine and let it evaporate over high heat for a minute or two.

Add the first ladleful of hot stock and, when the rice has absorbed all the liquid, pour in another ladleful of stock. Go on cooking in this way until the rice is nearly done (good Italian rice takes 18–20 minutes to cook.).

Chop together the anchovy fillets and garlic, and mix into the risotto, adding salt and pepper to taste. Mix well and continue cooking until the rice is done the way you like, and then serve.

BEAN AND VEGETABLE RISOTTO SOUP

Gluten free/milk-free/lactose-free

Anna says: This is a very rich, soupy risotto that must be made with dried beans and not tinned ones, because you need the flavour of the liquid in which they have cooked.

Michelle says: This is one of the dishes for which Anna was reluctant to allow me to suggest a meat free option as the flavour of the ham or bacon is a crucial part of the original recipe. But although a meat free version is obviously very different in flavour from the traditional dish, it still makes a great soup!!

If you can think far enough ahead to soak your beans overnight, this is not a hard-work dish. It just involves soaking and boiling – but it is very much worth it!

SERVES 5–6

INGREDIENTS

8 oz/225g dried borlotti or cannellini beans

1 knuckle of unsmoked bacon or ham
or
8 cups/3 pints/2 litres of well-flavoured, gluten free vegetable stock

1 bay leaf

1½ onions, chopped

1 medium carrot, diced

1 celery stick, diced

2 to 3 cabbage leaves, shredded

3 tbsp olive oil

1 garlic clove, finely chopped

1 small rosemary sprig, chopped

6 oz/170g coarse grain pure gluten free pork sausage, skinned and crumbled or

a well flavoured, coarse grained gluten free vegetarian sausage

10 oz/275g Italian rice (e.g. Arborio, Carnaroli, Vialone Nano)

½ cup/4fl oz/120ml red wine

1 tbsp tomato purée

sea salt and freshly ground black pepper

METHOD

Soak the beans overnight in cold water. Drain and rinse.

Put the beans, bacon (if you are using it), bay leaf, two-thirds of the onion, carrot, celery and cabbage leaves in a heavy-bottomed saucepan. Cover with about 2 litres of cold water – or, for the meat free version, the vegetable stock. Bring slowly to the boil. Simmer, covered, for about 3 hours (this can be done one or two days in advance; cool and chill until you are ready to use it).

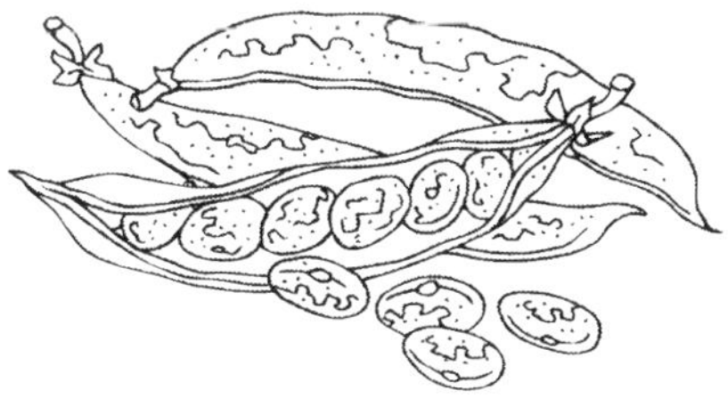

Leaving the soup to simmer, if you are using the ham or bacon knuckle, lift it out and remove the meat from the bone. Cut the meat into small pieces. Remove the bay leaf and discard.

If you are using meat add it, with the oil, garlic, rosemary, sausage and the remaining onion in a clean saucepan and fry gently for 5 minutes, stirring frequently. If you are not using meat then just fry the other ingredients together. Add the rice and mix well. Pour over the wine, boil briskly for 1 or 2 minutes, then add the tomato purée.

Pour over ¾ cup/6fl oz/180ml of the simmering soup and stir over a moderate heat. When the rice has absorbed nearly all the liquid, add another ½ cup/4fl oz/120ml of the soup. Keep stirring the rice, adding more soup as the rice dries out, but do not add too much soup at a time.

When the rice is cooked *al dente*, strain the soup and add any beans or pieces of vegetables left over in the stockpot to the risotto, and, if necessary, more liquid. This risotto should be rather liquid, halfway between a risotto and a soup.

Taste, season with salt and pepper, and serve.

RISOTTO WITH PRAWNS AND PEAS

Gluten free/can be milk-free

Anna says: A delicious and nourishing dish that you could produce at the last minute with ingredients you have in your freezer. Buy the best frozen prawns you can find – they have more flavour. The rest is easy.

Michelle says: If you want the risotto to be milk-free as well, eliminate the butter and use six tablespoons of olive oil in total.

SERVES 4

INGREDIENTS

2 oz/50g unsalted butter and 2 tbsp olive oil – or 6 tbsp olive oil

3 banana shallots, finely chopped

sea salt and black pepper

5 cups/2 pints/1.25 litres gluten free fish or vegetable stock

300g Italian rice (e.g. Arborio, Carnaroli, Vialone Nano)

1½ tsp gluten free curry powder, medium strength

3 tbsp dry sherry

5 oz/150g frozen petits pois

10 oz/300g frozen prawns

1–2 tsp lemon juice, to taste

METHOD

In a large and heavy saucepan, heat the butter and olive oil (or all of the oil). Throw in the shallots and cook over a moderate heat for 2–3 minutes. Sprinkle with some salt and continue cooking on a lower heat until the shallot is soft – another 4–5 minutes – stirring frequently.

Put the stock in a saucepan and bring to the boil. Keep it on the lowest possible heat as you cook the rice.

Add the rice to the shallots and sauté for 1–2 minutes while stirring constantly, so that all the grains absorb some of the butter and oil. Sprinkle with the curry powder, cook for a further minute, then splash with the sherry.

Cook, stirring constantly, until the sherry has been absorbed, then begin to pour in the stock a ladleful at a time, as with all the risottos. Do not add more liquid until the rice is beginning to get dry. If you finish the stock before the rice is properly cooked, just add boiling water.

About 10 minutes after you have begun adding the stock, throw in the petits pois. Mix well and cook for 5 minutes, then add the prawns and mix thoroughly. Season but be careful with the salt, because the fish stock might be already salted, and the prawns certainly are.

Cook until the rice is ready (good Italian rice cooks in about 18–20 minutes, depending on the variety).

Mix in the lemon juice, taste and adjust the seasoning. Serve at once.

TOMATOES STUFFED WITH RICE AND POTATOES

Gluten free/milk-free/lactose-free

Anna says: Dishes of lusciously coloured, stuffed vegetables are one of the joys of Italian cooking and always among them, are tomatoes. Try to get the big, knobbly, beef tomatoes, which have more flavour.

Michelle says: Another delicious, naturally free-from dish!

SERVES 6

INGREDIENTS

6 large, ripe but firm tomatoes, such as beef tomatoes, each weighing about 7oz/200g

sea salt and freshly ground black pepper

a pinch of flaked chilli

3 oz/80g uncooked Italian rice (e.g. Arborio, Carnaroli, Vialone Nano)

5 tbsp olive oil (with extra for greasing the dish)

1 garlic clove, chopped

6 canned anchovy fillets, rinsed and chopped

1 tbsp flat-leaf parsley, chopped

1 tbsp tomato purée

2 large potatoes, cut into very small cubes

2 tsp dried oregano

METHOD

Heat the oven to 350°F/180°C/Gas Mark 4.

Cut off the top of each tomato and reserve. Scoop the flesh and seeds out of the tomatoes, discard some of the seeds, chop the flesh into small pieces, and place it with the pulp in a bowl with a pinch of salt and the flaked chilli.

Add the rice, 3 tablespoons of the olive oil, garlic, anchovies, parsley and tomato purée. Mix thoroughly. Taste and adjust the seasoning to your liking.

Sprinkle the inside of the tomatoes with salt and fill them with the mixture. 'Lid' with the reserved tomato tops. Put the tomatoes in an oiled ovenproof dish into which they will fit comfortably, but not too loosely.

Put the cubed potato in a bowl, spoon over 1 tablespoon of the remaining olive oil and mix well to coat all the cubes, then arrange them around the tomatoes in the dish. Shower with the remaining 1 tablespoon of oil and oregano. Cook for about 1½ hours, or until the potato and rice are cooked, and serve.

MUSHROOM RISOTTO

Gluten free/can be milk-free/can be low lactose

Anna says: There are as many risotti con funghi in Northern Italy as there are cooks. This is one of my most used recipes, good and quite simple. I always add some dry porcini for added flavour.

Michelle says: Again, Anna would rather that you used butter for this dish, but if you do not eat milk products, substitute two tablespoons of olive oil for the butter when you cook the rice and leave out the Parmigiano-Reggiano.

SERVES 4

INGREDIENTS

½ oz/15g dried porcini

5 cups/2 pints/1.25 litres gluten free vegetable stock, or light chicken stock

3 tbsp olive oil

½ onion, very finely chopped

1 celery stalk, finely chopped

1 garlic clove, finely chopped

6 parsley sprigs, finely chopped

1 tbsp tomato purée

sea salt and freshly ground black pepper

8 oz/225g brown mushrooms, cleaned and sliced

2 oz/50g unsalted butter or 4 tbsp olive oil

12 oz/350g Italian rice (e.g. Arborio, Carnaroli, Vialone Nano)

$\frac{2}{3}$ cup/5fl oz/150ml dry white wine

freshly grated Parmigiano-Reggiano
(optional)

METHOD

To make the mushroom sauce:
Put the dried porcini in a bowl, cover with boiling water and set aside for about 20 minutes.

Heat the stock and keep it just simmering all through the cooking of the rice.

Heat the olive oil, with the onion, in a frying pan and cook gently for 2–3 minutes. Add the celery, garlic and parsley and sauté gently until the vegetables are soft, stirring frequently. Stir in the tomato paste and fry for a minute, then pour in a little stock. Continue cooking for about 5 minutes.

Remove the dried porcini from the liquid. Rinse them under cold water and dry them well. Chop them and add to the pan with a little more stock. Season with salt and pepper cook for about 2–3 minutes. Add the brown mushrooms and cook over high heat for a few minutes, then turn down the heat and continue cooking for a further 15 minutes, adding a little stock whenever there is no liquid in the pan. Set aside and keep warm.

For the rice:
Melt the butter (or heat the olive oil) in a heavy-bottomed saucepan. Add the rice and toast it for a minute or so, stirring constantly. Splash with the wine and let it evaporate while you continue stirring. Now add the simmering stock a ladleful at a time, allowing the liquid to be absorbed by the rice before you add the next ladleful (good Italian rice cooks in about 18–20 minutes, depending on the variety). If the rice is still not cooked but all the stock has been used, just add boiling water. About 15 minutes after you have begun to add the stock, spoon in 2 or 3 tablespoons of the mushroom sauce, mix well.

Once cooked, transfer the risotto to a warmed bowl or to warmed individual plates. Spoon the remaining mushroom sauce over the risotto and serve at once with a bowl of grated Parmigiano-Reggiano, if you are using it, on the side.

RICE WITH PEAS

Gluten free/can be milk-free/low lactose

Anna says: Neither a soup nor a risotto; this is one of the traditional dishes of the north eastern region of Italy, Veneto, where the peas are very small. Here we find sugar snap peas are the best variety to use but, if you cannot get sugar snaps, you can use a combination of mange tout and frozen petits pois.

Michelle says: To make this dish milk-free, substitute an extra two tablespoons of oil for the butter, and leave out the Parmigiano-Reggiano. If you are just avoiding lactose you may be able to eat the Parmigiano-Reggiano, as it is very low in lactose.

SERVES 4

INGREDIENTS

12 oz/300g mange tout

7 oz/200g frozen petits pois or 200g 2lb 4oz/1kg snap/sugar snap peas (in their pods)

2 tbsp olive oil and 2oz/50g unsalted butter – or 4 tbsp olive oil

1 banana shallot, very finely chopped

2 tbsp flat-leaf parsley, chopped

1 tsp sugar

10 oz/300g Italian rice (e.g. Arborio, Carnaroli, Vialone Nano)

sea salt and freshly ground black pepper

1 tbsp fennel seeds, crushed

2 oz/50g freshly grated Parmigiano-Reggiano (optional)

2 tbsp gluten free yeast flakes (optional)

METHOD

If you are using sugar snaps, pod the peas, keeping the pods and the peas separate. Wash the pods.

Put the sugar snap pods, or the mange tout if you are using them, in a saucepan, and add 8 cups/3 pints/2 litres of water and 2 tsp of salt. Bring to the boil and cook until the pods or mange tout are very tender. Drain, reserving the liquid.

Put the pods or mange tout in a food processor and process to a purée. Measure out 4 cups/1½ pints/1 litre of the cooking liquid and add it to the purée. Put the mixture into a saucepan and bring slowly to the boil.

Meanwhile, put the oil and butter (or just oil if you are not using butter) and shallot into a heavy-bottomed saucepan and sauté until the shallot is pale golden and soft. Mix in half the parsley, peas and sugar. Cook over a low heat for 2 minutes, stirring constantly.

Add the rice and cook, stirring constantly for 2 minutes, then pour in the stock and the pod purée.

Season with the fennel seeds, salt and a good grind of pepper. Cook, covered, until the rice is cooked (good Italian rice cooks in about 18–20 minutes, depending on the variety) – adding extra pea stock or water as needed. The texture should be a very sloppy risotto-cum-soup.

Turn off the heat and mix in the Parmigiano-Reggiano if you are using it. If you are not using the Parmigiano-Reggiano you could add extra flavour by mixing in 1–2 tbsp gluten free yeast flakes/nutritional yeast.

Taste and adjust the seasoning. Ladle the soup into individual bowls and sprinkle with the parsley. Serve immediately.

COMPRO
E
VENDO
LIBRI
USATI

OVEN-BAKED RISOTTO

Gluten free/can be milk-free/low lactose

Anna says: This is an odd hybrid dish, part-risotto, part-oven-cooked rice. The result is delicious.

Michelle says: To make this dish milk-free, use one tablespoon of oil instead of the butter, and leave out the Parmigiano-Reggiano. If you are just avoiding lactose, you may be able to eat the Parmigiano-Reggiano as it is very low in lactose.

SERVES 4

INGREDIENTS

1 or 2 shallots, or 1 small onion, finely chopped

3 tbsp olive oil

1 garlic clove, chopped

½ celery stick, chopped

½ carrot, chopped

8 oz/225g minced lean pork or minced Quorn or other meat substitute

½ cup/ 4fl oz/120ml dry white wine

2 cups/16fl oz/ 500ml gluten free meat or vegetable stock, depending on whether you are making the dish meat free or not

10 oz/300g Italian rice (e.g. Arborio, Carnaroli, Vialone Nano)

1 oz/5g butter, or 1 tbsp olive oil

4 tbsp freshly grated Parmigiano-Reggiano (optional)

sea salt and freshly ground black pepper

METHOD

Gently sauté the shallots in the olive oil until soft. Add the garlic, celery and carrot, and cook for 7 minutes, stirring frequently.

Mix in the pork or meat substitute and brown well. Splash in the wine, stir, then pour over about ½ cup/4fl oz/120ml of the stock. Cover the pan and simmer for about 1 hour, stirring every now and then, and adding a little more stock if necessary.

Heat the oven to 400°F/200°C/Gas Mark 6.

Cook the rice in salted boiling water for 7–8 minutes. Drain and add to the meat together with the remaining stock. Bring to the boil, then add the butter (or oil) and Parmigiano-Reggiano, if you are using it. Mix thoroughly and transfer to a buttered or oiled ovenproof dish.

Bake for 15–20 minutes or so until a light crust has formed on the top. Serve with a bowl of Parmigiano-Reggiano on the side. (Optional)

RICE AND ZUCCHINI/COURGETTE TORTA

Gluten free/low lactose

Anna says: This is delicious hot, or at room temperature, but neither straight from the oven nor the fridge. We served it with a green salad, and it was perfect; a tomato salad dressed with olive oil and lemon juice would be very good too. The torta also works made with leeks instead of zucchini/courgettes (in this case, eliminate the shallots and increase the quantity of the leeks to 1 lb 8 oz/750g).

Michelle says: The torta does depend heavily on Parmigiano Reggiano for its flavour, so it would be hard to leave it out but, if you are lactose, rather than milk intolerant, you may be able to eat it anyhow as the Parmigiano-Reggiano is very low in lactose.

SERVES 4

INGREDIENTS

1lb/500g zucchini/courgettes, cut into matchsticks

3 banana shallots, thinly sliced

6 oz/70g Italian rice (e.g. Arborio, Carnaroli, Vialone Nano)

4–5 tbsp olive oil (with extra for greasing the tin)

3 eggs

6 tbsp freshly grated Parmigiano Reggiano

a pinch of saffron strands

1 tsp of caster sugar

sea salt and freshly ground black pepper

⅔ cup/5fl oz/150ml gluten free vegetable stock

METHOD

Put the zucchini/courgettes, shallots and rice in a bowl. Add the olive oil and mix thoroughly, using two forks: they are better than spoons for amalgamating the various ingredients.

In a separate, small bowl, lightly beat the eggs together, mix in the cheese, and add to the bowl with the rice mixture. Mix thoroughly.

Place the saffron strands into a mortar, add the sugar and pound with the pestle until the saffron is all broken up. Using a pastry brush, add it to the rice mixture (a pastry brush will get the saffron out of the bowl more easily than a spoon will). Pour ½ tablespoon of hot water into the mortar, shake the water around and then pour it into the bowl with the rice – saffron is more precious than gold dust; you don't want to waste any.

Mix the whole thing thoroughly with the two forks, and season with salt and pepper. Then cover the bowl with a cloth and set aside for about two hours but remember to mix every now and then so that all the rice gets the chance to soak and soften in the liquid.

Preheat the oven to 350°F/180°C/Gas Mark 4.

Oil a 7 inch/18cm springform or loose bottomed cake tin, line with parchment paper, then oil the paper. Spoon the mixture into the tin, cover and bake for about 1 hour 10 minutes until the rice is cooked—you can scrape a few grains off the top and taste. About halfway through the cooking time, pour the stock slowly over the top of the dish, allowing it to soak in.

Leave the torta in the tin for about 5 minutes, then unmould, peel off the paper and serve.

PULSES

Tuscan bean soup—La Ribollita – **GF/MF/LF**

Lentils with sausage (meat or veggie) and mushrooms – **GF/MF/LF**

Chickpeas with rocket, chilli and garlic – **GF/MF/LF**

Cannellini beans sautéed in garlic oil – **GF/MF/LF**

Broad bean purée with radicchio and spring onions – **GF/MF/LF**

Polenta with pesto – **GF/can be MF/can be LF**

LENTILS WITH SAUSAGE (MEAT OR VEGGIE) AND MUSHROOMS

Gluten free/milk-free/lactose-free

Anna says: An all-in-one meal, as delicious as it is nourishing.

Michelle says: The original recipe was served with Parmigiano-Reggiano, but the dish has so much flavour that we really didn't think that it was needed.

SERVES 6

INGREDIENTS

12 oz/350g continental or green lentils

2 bay leaves

14 oz/110g unsmoked pancetta (bacon) cubes or, if you want it to be meat free, 6 anchovies or 3 slices of 'veggie bacon'

4 tbsp olive oil

1 onion, finely chopped

1 celery stick, finely chopped

1 carrot, finely chopped

1 lb/450g Italian Luganega sausage or other coarse-grained, gluten free pure pork sausages, skinned and cut into chunks – or, if you do not want to eat meat, 1lb/450g coarse vegetarian sausages

½ cup/4fl oz/120ml red wine

1 x 14 oz/400g can chopped plum tomatoes (with juice)

sea salt and freshly ground black pepper

1 garlic clove, peeled and lightly crushed

8 oz/225g brown mushrooms, cleaned and sliced

METHOD

First, cook the lentils with the bay leaves and a little salt in plenty of boiling water for about 10 minutes. Drain the lentils, reserving a mugful or so of the liquid,

In a large sauté pan, fry the pancetta/bacon (or the anchovies/veggie bacon) in 1 tablespoon of the olive oil for 2 minutes, then add the onion, celery and carrot and continue frying until soft – about 7–8 minutes. Add the sausages and sauté for 5 minutes, breaking them up with a fork and turning them over and over so that they brown on all sides.

Pour over the wine, raise the heat, and boil fast for a minute or two. Add the tomatoes and their juice, and season. Stir, cover the pan and simmer for 30 minutes or so. If the sauce gets too dry during the cooking, add some of the lentil liquid.

Mix in the lentils and continue cooking, covered, over low heat, for some 20 minutes, stirring occasionally. Taste and adjust the seasoning.

While the sausage and lentils are cooking, make the mushroom sauce.

To make the mushroom sauce:
Put the remaining olive oil and the crushed garlic into a frying pan over a low heat. When the oil is hot, add the brown mushrooms and sauté for some 15 minutes, stirring frequently. Remove the garlic and discard, then add salt and pepper to taste.

Mix the mushrooms into the lentil mixture and cook all together for a couple of minutes, then serve.

CHICKPEAS WITH ARUGULA/ROCKET, CHILLI AND GARLIC

Gluten free/milk-free/lactose-free

Anna says: A simple, classic recipe from Southern Italy, perfect for tinned chickpeas.

Michelle says: And naturally milk-free too!

SERVES 4

INGREDIENTS

4 garlic cloves

5 tbsp olive oil

1 fresh chilli, deseeded and finely chopped

2 x 14 oz/400g tins chickpeas, drained and rinsed

approx. 1 oz/25g arugula/rocket

sea salt

a few tbsp gluten free vegetable stock

freshly ground black pepper

METHOD

Chop 2 of the garlic cloves finely, and push a wooden cocktail stick through the other 2 so that you can fish them out easily when the sauce is done. Or, if you like a very garlicky sauce, chop them all.

Heat the olive oil in a large sauté pan, add the garlic and the chilli and sauté for 1 minute. Add the chickpeas and gently heat them in the oil, turning them over and over so that they all get coated with the oil. Add 2 or 3 tablespoons of the stock to moisten them and cook for about 5–8 minutes, adding stock whenever necessary.

Put the rocket in a bowl and add the hot chickpeas with all their juices. Fish out any whole garlic cloves and discard. Mix well, check the salt, and serve warm or at room temperature.

BROCCOLETTI WITH PULSES

Gluten free/milk-free/lactose-free

Anna says: A lovely combination of vegetables and pulses in a filling 'stew'.

Michelle says: All naturally 'free-from'...

SERVES 4–6

INGREDIENTS

4 oz/110g Puy or Castelluccio lentils

1 bay leaf

½ cup/4fl oz/120ml extra virgin olive oil

1 large red onion, chopped

10 oz/300g cherry tomatoes, peeled and halved

1 clove garlic, chopped

2–3 tsp chilli flakes

1 x 7 oz/200g can chickpeas, drained

1 x 7 oz/200g can cannellini beans, drained

6 oz/170g frozen petits pois

1 lb 2 oz/500g broccoletti/tenderstem broccoli

sea salt

METHOD

Drain the chickpeas and cannellini beans.

Put the lentils in a saucepan and add 1 cup/8fl oz/250ml water and the bay leaf. Bring to the boil and cook until tender – approximately 20 minutes. Strain but keep the liquid.

Heat 4 tablespoons of the oil in a large frying pan and when hot, add the onion, tomato, garlic and chilli. Cook over a lively heat for 10 minutes breaking up the tomatoes with the back of a spoon. Add the chickpeas, cannellini beans and lentils and cook gently for 5–8 minutes, stirring occasionally. Add the petits pois and continue to cook until they have defrosted and warmed in the sauce.

Meanwhile, wash the broccoletti/tenderstem broccoli and cook for 5 minutes in a pan full of boiling salted water. Drain and add to the pan with the pulses. Add 3–4 tablespoons of the lentil water then pour in the remaining oil. Mix well, check the seasoning and serve.

CANNELLINI BEANS SAUTÉED IN GARLIC OIL

Gluten free/milk-free/lactose-free

Anna says: This classic dish can be made with or without tomatoes. I prefer the simpler, older version without the tomatoes, as the flavour or the beans comes through more strongly. If you prefer the tomato version add 400g/14 oz peeled and chopped tomatoes to the garlicky oil and cook for 15 minutes over a lively heat before adding the beans.

Michelle says: I am with Anna for the tomato free version! This is also delightfully quick to make.

SERVES 4

INGREDIENTS

3 garlic cloves

4 tbsp extra virgin olive oil

12 sage leaves, coarsely torn

1–2 pinches of chilli flakes

2 x14 oz/200g cans cannellini beans

sea salt

METHOD

Chop the garlic cloves. If the garlic is old, cut the cloves in half and remove the germ before chopping – this will make the garlic sweeter. Put the garlic in a frying pan with the oil, sage and chilli and fry gently until it begins to colour.

Drain and rinse the cannellini beans and add to the frying pan. Mix well and cook over a low heat for 5 minutes, stirring frequently. Taste, add salt if necessary – and serve.

BROAD BEAN PURÉE WITH RADICCHIO AND SPRING ONIONS

Gluten free/milk-free/lactose-free

Anna says: You need dried broad beans for this recipe, which you can buy in good supermarkets or in any Italian or Middle Eastern deli. The dish comes from Puglia, in the south-eastern tip of Italy. There, they use the local chicory which has a somewhat bitterer flavour than radicchio, but it is very hard to find outside Puglia. Red radicchio makes a very good – and pretty – substitute.

Michelle says: Delicious – and naturally free-from.

SERVES 4

INGREDIENTS

7 oz/200g dried broad/fava beans

7 oz/200g waxy potatoes

1 bunch scallions/spring onions

2 medium heads red radicchio

6 tbsp extra virgin olive oil

2 tsp wine vinegar

4 oz/110g green olives, stoned/pitted but not dressed

2 bay leaves

sea salt and freshly ground black pepper

METHOD

Soak the beans in water for 1 hour and drain. If you have one, put them in an earthenware casserole dish you can put on the heat, otherwise in a heavy saucepan.

Peel the potatoes and cut into chunks. Add to the beans and cover both with water, adding 1 teaspoon of salt. Bring to the boil, turn down the heat to simmer and cook for 1 hour.

Meanwhile, cut the green tops off the scallions/spring onions, keeping only the pale green leaves and white bulbs. Wash and cut them into ½ inch/1 cm strips and set aside. Cut the radicchio in half and then into segments. Wash and cook it in boiling salted water for 5 minutes and then drain.

When the beans and potatoes are cooked, drain them and transfer to a food processor. Whizz to a coarse purée and then scoop into a serving bowl.

Heat the remaining oil in a small pan and when hot, throw in the olives and the bay leaves. Cook for 5 minutes, shaking the pan frequently. Remove from the heat and discard the bay leaves.

Mix the radicchio with the spring onions, 3 tbsp of oil, the vinegar, salt and pepper then mix in the olives and cooking juices. Serve immediately with the broad bean purée.

POLENTA WITH PESTO

Gluten free/can be milk-free/can be lactose-free

Anna says: In Liguria, north-western Italy, pesto is added to lasagne, layered with the local soft cheese. In this dish Michelle and I are using polenta, in the same way as lasagne, and it works really well.

Michelle says: Those on milk-free diets might want to try this dish using a milk-free pesto and one of the many new nut-based cheeses. Alternatively, you could make it just with the pesto and the walnuts, both of which have lots of flavour of their own.

SERVES 4–6

INGREDIENTS

10 oz/275g quick cook/instant polenta

freshly ground black pepper

4 tbsp olive oil

9 oz/250g gluten free basil or tomato pesto (if the dish is to be milk-free you need to use a milk/dairy-free pesto)

4 oz/110g chopped walnuts

14 oz/400g mozzarella (optional)

4 oz/110g Pecorino Romano, grated (optional)

METHOD

Start by making the polenta following the instructions on the pack.

Pour the cooked polenta onto a wooden board and spread it out to a thickness of approximately 2 inches/8cm. Allow to cool for at least 2 hours.

Preheat the oven to 400°F/200°C/Gas Mark 6). Grease a 10 x 7 inch/25cm x 18cm baking dish – a lasagne dish is ideal – with 1 tablespoon of the olive oil.

When the polenta is cold, cut it into ¾ inch/20cm thick slices, and cover the base of the tin with approximately half of them. Season with pepper, drizzle with 1 tablespoon of the oil, then spread the pesto over the polenta pieces.

Set aside 2 tablespoons of the walnuts and sprinkle the remainder over the pesto. Cover with half the mozzarella, torn into pieces, and half the Pecorino Romano. Layer the remaining polenta on top, sprinkle 1 tablespoon of the oil over it, and then top with the remaining mozzarella cut into slices.

Sprinkle with the remaining pecorino, walnuts and olive oil, and a generous grind of pepper.

Cover the dish with foil and bake for about 20 minutes. Remove the foil and bake for a further 10 minutes, until a lovely gold crust has formed on the top and serve.

TUSCAN BEAN SOUP—LA RIBOLLITA

Gluten free/milk-free/lactose-free

Anna says: Ribollita means 'boiled again'. This Tuscan soup should be made at least a day in advance, in order to allow all the flavours to mingle and mix together. It is traditionally ladled onto toasted bread, but it is also excellent without it.

I am afraid tinned beans are not suitable for this soup because you need the flavour that the dried beans give to the liquid in which they are cooked.

Michelle says: This soup is worth the effort of thinking ahead and soaking the beans – and it is naturally, totally free-from!

SERVES 6

INGREDIENTS

8 oz/225g dried cannellini beans

6 tbsp olive oil

1 onion, finely chopped

1 carrot, chopped

1 celery stick, chopped

2 leeks, very finely sliced

2 ripe tomatoes, peeled, seeded and chopped

1 sprig of fresh rosemary, chopped

6 garlic cloves, peeled and finely chopped

1 sprig of fresh thyme

flaked chilli, to taste

9 oz/250g Cavolo Nero, stalks discarded and leaves finely sliced

sea salt and freshly ground black pepper

2 red onions, very finely sliced

1 slice coarse gluten free bread per person (optional)

METHOD

Soak the beans overnight. Drain and rinse them.

Choose a heavy stockpot (preferably earthenware) and put 2 tablespoons of the olive oil into it. Heat, add the onion and after 5 minutes, add the carrot, celery, leeks, tomatoes, rosemary and half the garlic.

Sauté for 10 minutes, stirring frequently. Add the beans and turn them over and over to coat them in the oil. Cover with 8 cups/2½ pints/2 litres of water, add salt and cook, covered, at the gentlest simmer for at least 2 hours, until the beans are very soft

Lift out half of the beans and purée them in a food processor. Return the purée to the soup and stir well. Ideally, the soup will now rest overnight, so you can cool and chill it at this point until you are ready.

Bring the soup back to a simmer and preheat the oven to 350°F/180°C/Gas Mark 4.

Heat all but 1 tablespoon of the remaining oil in a small frying pan. Add the remaining garlic, thyme and chilli and sauté gently for about 2 minutes, stirring constantly and being very careful not to let the garlic burn.

Mix this into the soup, then add the Cavolo Nero. Taste and adjust the seasoning. Scatter the sliced red onion over the top of the soup and drizzle with the remaining oil.

Cover the soup and place in the oven for 45 minutes to 1 hour; if you are using the onion, it should be soft.

If you are using the toasted bread, put a slice in the bottom of each bowl and ladle the soup over it. If you are not using the toast, just ladle the soup into bowls and serve.

BAR

VEGETABLE DISHES

Artichokes with peas – **GF/MF/LF**

Asparagus with fried eggs and Parmigiano-Reggiano – **GF/can be MF/can be LL**

Tipsy cabbage – **GF/MF/LF**

Carrots in wine and herb sauce – **GF/MF/LF**

Cauliflower stewed in wine – **GF/MF/LF**

Cavolo Nero and potatoes sautéed with chilli and garlic – **GF/MF/LF**

Celeriac and eggplant/aubergine in tomato sauce – **GF/MF/LF**

Hard boiled eggs with arugula/rocket and tomato sauce – **GF/MF/LF**

Eggplant/aubergine with a hundred flavours – **GF/MF/LF**

Eggplant/aubergine pizzas – **GF/can be MF/can be LF**

Baked green beans and porcini polpettone – **GF/can be MF/can be LF**

Baked onion frittata – **GF/can be MF/can be LF or LL**

Peas and mushrooms with marjoram – **GF/can be MF/can be LF**

Grilled peppers with anchovies, olives and capers – **GF/MF/LF**

Pepperonata or Pepper and tomato ratatouille – **GF/MF/LF**

Potato and zucchini/courgette frittata – **GF/can be MF/LL**

Grilled red radicchio with endive/chicory – **GF/MF/LF**

ARTICHOKES WITH PEAS

Gluten free/milk-free/lactose-free

Anna says: This a traditional recipe from Rome, prepared in the spring with the first peas and the first Romanesco artichokes.

Michelle says: What is not like about this? Delicious and totally free-from.

SERVES 4

INGREDIENTS

4 tender young globe artichokes

lemon juice

2 shallots or 1 small onion, finely chopped

2 oz/50g prosciutto/Parma ham finely chopped

4 tbsp olive oil

⅔ cup/5fl oz/150ml gluten free vegetable stock

10 oz/300g shelled fresh garden peas or frozen petits pois

sea salt and freshly ground black pepper

METHOD

Prepare the artichokes by discarding the tough outer leaves, cutting off about 1 inch/3cm from the top and removing the stalks. Plunge the artichokes into cold water, into which you have added 1 tablespoon of lemon juice, to prevent them turning black.

Put the shallots and prosciutto/Parma ham into a heavy saucepan with the olive oil. Sauté gently while you cut the artichokes in half, removing the furry chokes and then, unless they are very small, cut them into quarters. Dry them and add to the pan. Cook over a low heat for about 5 minutes, turning them continually.

Pour the stock over the artichokes, add the peas (fresh or frozen) with a little salt and pepper. Cook until the artichokes are tender – you may need to add a couple of tablespoons of water if it seems too dry.

Check seasoning and serve.

ASPARAGUS WITH FRIED EGGS AND PARMIGIANO-REGGIANO

Gluten free/can be milk-free/can be low lactose

Anna says: This is my favourite supper dish when the first fresh asparagus of the season appears. In Italy, many people prefer white asparagus and claim priority for their local variety. My personal favourite is young and green! You also need good cheese for this recipe, or the flavour of the cheese will kill the asparagus rather than combining with it.

Michelle says: If you wanted to make this dish milk-free, substitute olive oil for the butter and leave out the cheese. The combination of the fresh asparagus and the eggs will still be delicious.

SERVES 4

INGREDIENTS

3lbs/1.4 kilo fresh young asparagus spears

sea salt

2 oz/50g unsalted butter or 3–4 tbsp extra virgin olive oil

4 tbsp freshly grated Parmigiano-Reggiano

8 free range eggs

freshly ground black pepper

fresh, crusty, gluten free bread

METHOD

Cut off the hard part of the asparagus stems. Wash thoroughly.

If you have a tall saucepan, tie the asparagus in small bundles (tying them at the tip and the bottom) and stand them upright in the saucepan, then half fill the saucepan with boiling water and salt well. The feet of the asparagus should be in the water and the heads cooking in the steam. If you do not have a tall enough pan you can also lay the spears out in a sauté pan, or deep, frying pan and half fill the pan with boiling salted water.

In either case, cook on a moderate heat for 5–8 minutes or until the spears give easily to the point of a sharp knife. Remove from the pan and drain thoroughly.

Dry the asparagus and place on individual plates.

Melt ¾ of the butter and pour it over the asparagus spears – or pour over half the olive oil.

Sprinkle with the Parmigiano-Reggiano if you are using it.

Melt the remaining butter, or heat the remaining oil, in a non-stick pan and break in the eggs.

When fried, slide the eggs onto the plates with the asparagus and grind over lots of black pepper.

Serve at once with crusty, gluten free bread.

TIPSY CABBAGE

Gluten free/milk-free/lactose-free

Anna says: Cabbage is often cooked in wine in the Trentino and other mountainous regions of northern Italy, which were part of the Austro-Hungarian empire – just think of sauerkraut. Instead of the red cabbage I have used, you could also use a pointed cabbage or a Savoy cabbage.

Michelle says: Another delicious naturally free-from vegetable dish.

SERVES 4

INGREDIENTS

1 medium sized red cabbage

1 medium onion

the needles from 2 generous sprigs of rosemary

2 garlic cloves

2 tbsp olive oil

¾ cup/6fl oz/120ml red or white wine, depending on what you have available and your preference

sea salt and freshly ground black pepper

METHOD

Cut the cabbage in half, and then in quarters, and remove the hard core. Cut the quarters into thin shreds and wash and drain them. The easiest way to wash shredded cabbage is to put it into a colander and place the colander in a sink full of water. Give it a good swish around and then lift the colander out of the sink and allow to drain.

Chop the rosemary and garlic together. Place the mixture into a large pan and add the oil. Cook for 5 minutes and then add the cabbage, a few handfuls at a time so that you can mix it well. When all the cabbage is in, add the wine.

Season with salt and pepper, cover and cook gently over a low heat for 40–60 minutes depending on how cooked or crunchy you like your cabbage – and checking regularly to make sure it is not too dry. If needed add a little extra water.

When cooked, season to taste and serve.

CARROTS IN WINE AND HERB SAUCE

Gluten free/milk-free/lactose-free

Anna says: Carrots, which in Britain are particularly good, are, I think, a very underrated vegetable.

Michelle says: Carrots are also one of the least allergenic vegetables around.

SERVES 4

INGREDIENTS

1 lb 4 oz/550g carrots

4 tbsp olive oil

¾ cup/6fl oz/180ml dry white wine

3 tbsp white wine vinegar

2 sprigs flat-leaf parsley

2 sprigs fresh thyme

3 fresh sage leaves

2 bay leaves

3 sprigs fresh mint

1 large/2 small cloves garlic, cut in half

sea salt and freshly ground black pepper

1 tbsp superfine/caster sugar

METHOD

Cut the carrots into thick matchsticks and add to a sauté pan.

Add all the other ingredients, plus ½ cup/4fl oz/120ml water. Bring to the boil and cook uncovered for 30 minutes. The carrots will still be quite crunchy. Lift the carrots out with a slotted spoon and set aside.

Boil the liquid rapidly to reduce until it is a beautiful deep gold colour. Most of the water will have evaporated and you will be left with a delicious, hot, herby vinaigrette. Taste and adjust seasoning. Pour the reduced liquid over the carrots and leave to marinate for up to 48 hours.

Remove the herbs and garlic before serving and serve at room temperature.

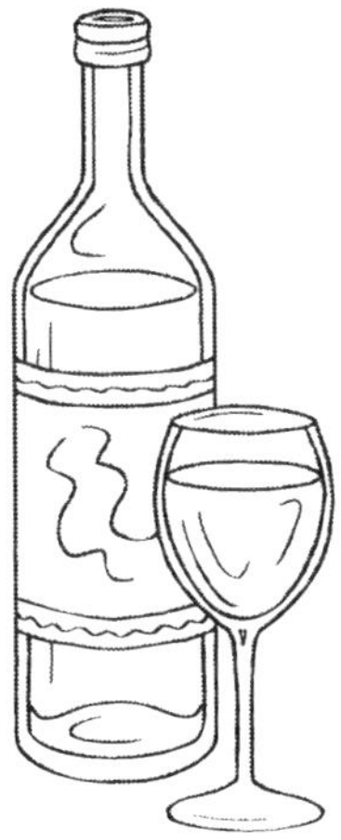

CAULIFLOWER STEWED IN WINE

Gluten free/milk-free/lactose-free

Anna says: Cauliflower is one of my favourite vegetables, especially cooked in wine!

Michelle says: Another naturally free-from recipe...

SERVES 4

INGREDIENTS

1 cauliflower, approx. 1lb 8oz/700g in weight, with the coarse outer leaves and central stalk removed

1 oz/25g flat-leaf parsley

1 garlic clove

5 tbsp olive oil

½ tsp chilli flakes

2/3 cup/5fl oz/150ml dry white wine

METHOD

Cut the cauliflower into quarters and then into florets; wash and drain them.

Remove the tough stalks from the parsley and chop together with the garlic.

Pour the oil into a sauté pan, add 2 tablespoons of the parsley and garlic mixture and the chilli and cook until the garlic is fragrant. Mix in the cauliflower florets and sauté gently for 3–4 minutes turning them regularly. Add enough boiling water to come 1 inch/2.5 cm up the pan. Cover with a lid and cook for 5 minutes.

Pour in the wine and continue to cook gently, uncovered until the cauliflower is cooked – approximately 20 minutes although it is difficult to be specific about the time as it will depend on the size of the florets and how *al dente* you like your vegetables.

When it is cooked to your liking, taste and add salt if needed. It should not need any pepper because of the chilli flakes. Serve at once.

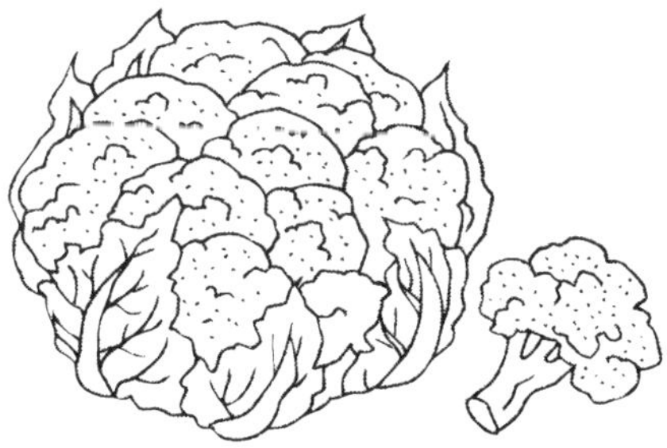

CAVOLO NERO AND POTATOES SAUTÉED WITH CHILLI AND GARLIC

Gluten free/milk-free/lactose-free

Anna says: In this dish the potatoes lend substance to the Cavolo Nero and the Cavolo Nero lends its peculiar, bitter-cabbagey flavour to the potatoes – a delicious combination.

Michelle says: So simple, but a tasty combination indeed. For those who don't know Cavolo Nero it is a cabbage with long, dark green crinkly leaves and a rather special flavour. If you cannot find it, you could still make this dish with a crinkly Savoy cabbage or even with curly kale.

SERVES 4

INGREDIENTS

4 large waxy potatoes, approx. 1 lb 8 oz/700g

10 Cavolo Nero leaves

6 tbsp olive oil

2 garlic cloves

2 pinches chilli flakes

sea salt

METHOD

Scrub the potatoes and put them, still in their skins, in a saucepan. Cover with cold water, add 1 tablespoon of salt and cook at a lively simmer until just tender when tested with the point of a small knife. Lift them out of the water with a slotted spoon (do not throw the water out) and place in a colander until cool enough to peel. Peel and cut into large bite-sized chunks.

Remove the tougher ends of the stalks of the Cavolo Nero, wash the leaves and cut into strips. Bring the potato water back to the boil and add the Cavolo Nero. Boil until tender – it will take 10–15 minutes. Drain well.

While the Cavolo Nero is cooking, heat the oil in a large frying pan and add the garlic and chilli flakes. Sauté until just golden and add the potatoes. Mix well for a minute or two and then add the Cavolo Nero and continue cooking for 5 minutes, turning all the time.

Taste and add salt if necessary and serve.

CELERIAC AND EGGPLANT/AUBERGINE BRAISED IN TOMATO SAUCE

Gluten free/milk-free/lactose-free

Anna says: This recipe combines two vegetables which, on paper, sound as though they should never be brought together but in fact make an extraordinarily good combination of flavours.

Michelle says: A really delicious combination and makes a very good meal on its own.

SERVES 4

INGREDIENTS

1 small **celeriac**, approx. 1 lb 8 oz/700g

1 large **eggplant/aubergine**, approx. 12 oz/350g

5 tbsp **olive oil**

1 oz/25g **flat-leaf parsley leaves**

1 **garlic clove**, chopped

1 tbsp **tomato paste/purée**

Scant ½ cup/3fl oz/90ml **gluten free vegetable stock**

sea salt and freshly ground **black pepper**

METHOD

Heat the oven to 350°F/180°C/Gas mark 4.

Peel the celeriac and cut into 1 inch/2cm cubes. Wash the eggplant/aubergine and cut into similar size cubes. Put them both in a bowl and pour over 1tablespoon of olive oil. Mix together with your hands and make sure that the vegetables are well coated in the oil.

Heat the remaining oil in a pan that you will be able to put into the oven. Add the flat-leaf parsley and garlic and gently cook for a few minutes until the garlic starts to turn golden, then add the vegetable cubes. Mix well, turning the vegetable cubes over and over, and cook gently for 3–4 minutes. Add the tomato purée and continue cooking for a further 2–3 minutes. Pour in about half of the stock, mix well, season with salt and pepper and bring to the boil.

Cover the pan and put it in the oven. Cook until the vegetables are done which will take 30–40 minutes. If necessary, add a little more stock. The vegetables should cook in a little liquid, but they should be fairly dry when they are ready.

Serve hot.

HARD BOILED EGGS WITH ARUGULA/ROCKET AND TOMATO SAUCE

Gluten free/milk-free/lactose-free

Anna says: I first had this sauce many years ago created by Angelo Paracucchi at his restaurant in Sarzana in Liguria, north-west Italy. Angelo served it with boiled fish or meat but my favourite way to eat it is with hard boiled eggs. The arugula/rocket does lose some of its pungency through being combined with the tomato – and it is not that pretty a colour – but it tastes most appealing, sweet and herby at the same time.

Michelle says: And totally free-from – what is not to like?

SERVES 4

INGREDIENTS

1 oz/30g arugula/rocket

7 oz/200g firm and slightly under ripe tomatoes

sliver of peeled garlic

1 small green chilli, de-seeded

1 tbsp balsamic vinegar

sea salt and freshly ground black pepper

5 tbsp extra virgin olive oil

8 eggs

METHOD

Wash the arugula/rocket and dry carefully. Remove any tough stalks and put the leaves in a food processor.

Blanch the tomatoes for 1 minute in boiling water, then plunge into cold water. Peel the tomatoes, quarter them, discard the seeds and squeeze out the juice.

Add the tomatoes to the arugula/rocket in the processor along with the garlic, chilli, vinegar and a little salt and pepper. Process for 15 seconds then continue to process, gradually adding the oil as for mayonnaise. Adjust the seasoning to taste.

Meanwhile, boil the eggs for between 5–8 minutes depending on the size of the eggs and how hard/soft you want the yolks to be.

Remove the eggs from the boiling water and plunge into cold. Allow to cool and then peel.

Serve the eggs with the sauce and either a green salad or crusty, gluten free bread or toast.

EGGPLANT/AUBERGINE WITH A HUNDRED FLAVOURS

Gluten free/milk-free/lactose-free

Anna says: This dish is the Calabrian answer to the famous caponata dish from Sicily and contains, as does its Sicilian counterpart, a little bitter chocolate.

Michelle says: Even though there are a lot of ingredients in this delicious dish, I am delighted to say that none of them contain gluten or dairy products.

SERVES 4

INGREDIENTS

2 oz/50g golden raisins/sultanas

1 lb 8 oz/700g eggplant/aubergines

2 celery stalks

6 tbsp olive oil

1 onion, finely chopped

2 garlic cloves, finely chopped

2 tbsp soft brown sugar

3–4 tbsp wine vinegar

1 oz/25g walnuts, chopped

1 oz/25g pine kernels/pine nuts

1 oz/25g dark, milk-free chocolate

sea salt and freshly ground black pepper

METHOD

Put the sultanas in a bowl, cover with boiling water and leave to plump up for 20 minutes. Drain and dry them.

Remove the ends of the eggplants/aubergines and discard. Wash them well and cut them into small cubes of approximately ¾ inch/2cm. Remove the outside strings from the celery and cut it into pieces around the same size as the eggplant/aubergine.

Take a large sauté pan and add the oil. When it is hot, add the onion and garlic and cook gently for 5 minutes. Add the eggplant/aubergine and celery and cook for a further 10 minutes over a lively heat, stirring frequently and being sure that the vegetables do not catch on the bottom of the pan.

Add the sugar and let the vegetables caramelise a bit before you add the vinegar. Cook for 5 minutes, stirring frequently, then add the walnuts, pine nuts, golden raisins/sultanas and salt and pepper to taste. Mix well and continue cooking over a lively heat for a further 5 minutes, stirring frequently, or until the eggplant/aubergines take on a golden hue.

Flake the chocolate directly over the pan – I find it easier to use a small knife than to grate it. Stir again and turn the heat down. Cover and cook gently for around 45 minutes until the eggplant/aubergines are soft but the celery still has a little bite. During the cooking, keep a watch and add a little water as necessary. The vegetables should always cook in a little liquid and never dry out.

Taste and adjust the seasoning if necessary, before serving.

EGGPLANT/AUBERGINE PIZZAS

Gluten free/can be milk-free/can be lactose-free

Anna says: I love this dish. The similarity with pizza lies in its topping which is piled on top of the eggplant/aubergine instead of the pizza dough. The eggplant/aubergine can be roasted in a hot oven for 5 minutes or steamed, as in this recipe.

Michelle says: What is not to love about this? A naturally gluten free pizza!! If you want to make it milk-free as well, substitute a soft vegan cheese (in some places you can now even find a vegan mozzarella) for the buffalo mozzarella. Of course, if you are only avoiding cow's milk, you will be fine with buffalo mozzarella.

SERVES 4

INGREDIENTS

FOR THE SAUCE

1 x 4oz/100g tinned tomatoes

2 tbsp olive oil

1 garlic clove, crushed

1–2 pinches chilli flakes

2 pinches sea salt

FOR THE PIZZA BASE

3 medium eggplants/aubergines

Extra olive oil

9 oz/250g buffalo mozzarella

dried oregano

METHOD

Heat the oven to 350°F/180°C/Gas Mark 4.

Put the tomatoes, oil, garlic, chilli and salt into a saucepan and cook, uncovered, over a lively heat for about 15 minutes or until the oil has slightly separated from the tomatoes. Stir frequently and season to taste.

Remove the ends of the eggplants/aubergines, wash them and dry them. Cut each eggplant/aubergine into ½ inch/1 cm slices and either roast them in the oven for 5 minutes or put them in a steamer and steam until tender for around 5 minutes. How long this will take will depend on the size of your steamer so keep checking.

Brush a large baking sheet generously with some of the oil. Place the eggplant/aubergine slices on the sheet, brush each with more oil and sprinkle over a little salt.

Cut the mozzarella into ½ inch/1cm slices and lay over each eggplant/aubergine slice. Top with a level teaspoon of tomato sauce and sprinkle with a little oregano. Bake for 7–8 minutes and serve piping hot.

BAKED GREEN BEANS AND PORCINI POLPETTONE

Gluten free/can be milk-free/can be lactose-free

Anna says: A polpettone is a very traditional dish in Italy; a little bit of a bother to make but well worth the effort.

Michelle says: An easy dish to make gluten free – slightly harder to make milk-free although you could substitute soya or coconut milk and yogurt for the milk, and sour cream and vegan soft and hard cheese for the ricotta and Parmigiano-Reggiano.

SERVES 4 WITH PLENTY LEFT OVER FOR LUNCH THE NEXT DAY

INGREDIENTS

1 oz/25g dried porcini

1 lb/450g French or green beans

sea salt and freshly ground black pepper

2 oz/50g crustless, white gluten free bread – artisan if possible

scant ½ cup/3fl oz/90ml milk – cow or non-dairy of choice

5 tbsp extra virgin olive oil

2 cloves garlic finely chopped

1 tbsp chopped fresh marjoram

3 eggs

2 tbsp ricotta – or soft vegan cheese

4 tbsp sour cream – soya/coconut yogurt

2 oz/50 freshly grated Parmigiano-Reggiano – or grated hard vegan cheese

3 oz/75g dried white gluten free breadcrumbs

METHOD

Soak the porcini in hot water for an hour. If they are still gritty when you take them out, rinse them thoroughly and then dry them and chop them coarsely.

Top and tail the beans. Cook them in well salted water (beans need more salt than any other vegetable) for 5 minutes then drain, refresh under cold water and drain thoroughly. Chop them coarsely.

While the beans are cooking put the bread in a bowl with the milk and leave to soak.

Heat the oven to 350°F/180°C/Gas Mark 4.

Heat half the oil in a frying pan with the garlic and the marjoram. Add the porcini and beans and sauté for 2–3 minutes.

Squeeze the excess milk out of the bread and crumble it into the mixture. Continue to fry for a further 5 minutes, turning the whole thing over to take up the flavours.

Beat the eggs together lightly in a large bowl. Crumble the ricotta (or soft vegan cheese) and add to the eggs together with the sour cream (dairy-free yogurt), breadcrumbs, Parmigiano-Reggiano (hard vegan cheese) and lots of freshly ground black pepper. Mix well and then add the contents of the frying pan. Mix well again and adjust seasoning to taste.

Grease an 8 inch/20cm spring clip tin with a little extra oil. If you do not have a spring clip tin, line an 8 inch/20cm cake tin with greaseproof paper/baking parchment and oil. Sprinkle with enough breadcrumbs to coat the surface but tip any extra out.

Spoon the mixture into the tin. Flatten the top and pour over any extra oil Bake for 40 minutes or until a skewer comes out clean. Allow to partially cool in the tin and then unmould onto a round dish. Serve hot, warm, or at room temperature with a salad or crusty, gluten free bread. The polpettone is also excellent cold in slices for a picnic.

BAKED ONION FRITTATA

Gluten free/can be milk-free/can be lactose-free or low lactose

Anna says: This recipe comes from an old Italian friend of mine who like me, married an Englishman. Her recipes are always reliable.

Michelle says: There is a lot of Parmigiano-Reggiano in Myriam's original recipe and she uses butter as well as oil to cook the recipe. However, if you cook the onions slowly enough just in olive oil, they will have so much flavour of their own that you do not really need the Parmigiano-Reggiano at all! If you are on a low lactose diet, then you should be okay with the Parmigiano-Reggiano anyhow.

SERVES 4

INGREDIENTS

1 tbsp olive oil plus 1 tbsp unsalted butter – or 3 tbsp olive oil

1 lb 4 oz/550g onions, very finely sliced

8 eggs

2 tbsp freshly grated Parmigiano-Reggiano (optional)

sea salt and freshly ground black pepper

METHOD

Heat the oven to 350°F/180°C/Gas mark 4.

Heat the oil and butter if you are using butter, or just the oil, in a large sauté pan. Add the onions with a little salt to stop them burning, mix thoroughly and then cook very gently for 20–30 minutes, stirring regularly, until the onions are soft and golden. Do not stint on the cooking time as the longer you cook them, the more flavoursome they will be.

Break the eggs into a bowl and gently beat them. Season lightly with sea salt and freshly ground black pepper.

Grease an ovenproof dish (a lasagne dish is ideal) and spoon in the onions and their juices. Pour the beaten egg on top and bake for 25 minutes before serving.

If you are using Parmigiano-Reggiano, remove the dish from the oven, sprinkle the cheese over the top then put it under a hot grill just to brown the top.

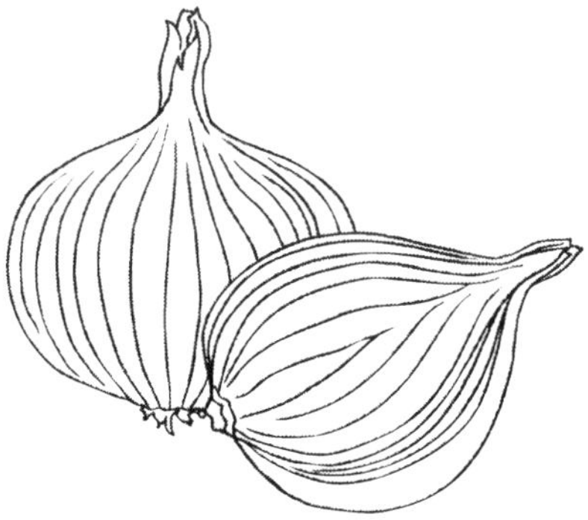

PEAS AND MUSHROOMS WITH MARJORAM

Gluten free/can be milk-free/can be lactose-free

Anna says: Peas are a good accompaniment to most meat, fish and meat alternative dishes. In this recipe their delicate flavour is enhanced by the addition of a few mushrooms and some fresh marjoram. Marjoram is such an easy herb to grow – mine is rapidly taking over one of the borders in my garden.

Michelle says: This lovely vegetable dish is really intended as accompaniment to meat or fish – but it is delicious as a light lunch dish with fresh, gluten free bread or even some lightly steamed new potatoes. The original used unsalted butter but it works just as well with olive oil.

SERVES 4

INGREDIENTS

4 tbsp extra virgin olive oil

1 shallot, finely chopped

sea salt

9 oz/250g button mushrooms, thickly sliced

12 oz/350g frozen petits pois

⅔ cup/5fl oz/150ml gluten free vegetable stock

freshly ground black pepper

1 tbsp chopped fresh marjoram leaves

METHOD

Heat the oil in a pan and add the shallots and a pinch of salt. Sauté for 2 minutes then add the mushrooms. Cook for 5 minutes, turning the mushrooms over frequently.

Add the stock and then the peas and cook until they are tender. If there is too much liquid in the pan when the peas are done, remove them with a slotted spoon into a dish and keep warm in a low oven. Then reduce the sauce to a syrupy consistency by boiling briskly over a high heat. Spoon the sauce over the peas and mushrooms, season with salt and pepper to taste and sprinkle with marjoram leaves before serving.

GRILLED PEPPERS WITH ANCHOVIES, OLIVES AND CAPERS

Gluten free/milk-free/lactose-free

Anna says: I love grilled peppers in every way, but these are particularly good thanks to the vinegary onion sauce in which they are finished off. For this dish, round peppers, not the long Romano ones, are better as they have a thicker skin.

Michelle says: Super tasty – and naturally free-from.

SERVES 4

INGREDIENTS

5 large red and yellow bell peppers

4 tbsp extra virgin olive oil

1 red onion, finely chopped

sea salt

2 garlic cloves, chopped

1 tsp gluten free vegetable stock powder

2 tbsp balsamic vinegar

1 tbsp superfine/caster sugar

freshly ground black pepper

1 tbsp dried oregano

16 black olives, pitted/de-stoned and cut into strips

6 canned anchovy fillets

2 tbsp capers, rinsed

METHOD

First you need to grill the peppers. The best way to do this is directly over a flame rather than under a broiler/grill. Put a wire rack on a gas ring then place one or two peppers straight onto it and leave until their skin has turned black. Turnover, char the other side and continue to turn and char until the whole pepper is blackish. But be careful not to leave the pepper in the same position for too long or it will burn through the skins and the pulp and you will have a hole! Repeat with the remaining peppers. If you do not have a direct flame put them under a broiler/grill and keep turning until they are blackish all over.

Remove the skins using your hands or a small knife. Don't wash the peppers or you will wash away their juices. Wipe the peppers with clean, damp kitchen towel/paper, cut them in half and then into quarters. Remove the cores and the seeds. Then cut them vertically into 1 inch/2cm strips. Now they are ready to be used.

Put the oil and onion in a frying pan, sprinkle with salt then add 2 tablespoons of water. Cook gently for about 15 minutes, stirring frequently, and then add the garlic and continue to cook for about 40 minutes or until the onion is like a golden mush.

Mix in the peppers, the bouillon powder, vinegar, sugar and pepper to taste and cook over a gentle heat for 20 minutes, turning the whole thing over now and then. If the mixture gets too dry add a couple of tablespoons of hot water.

Add the oregano, olives, anchovies and capers, mix well and continue cooking over a low heat for 10 minutes. Serve warm or at room temperature with crusty, gluten free bread.

PEPPERONATA OR PEPPER AND TOMATO RATATOUILLE

Gluten free/milk-free/lactose-free

Anna says: When I was a child in Milan, pepperonata always appeared on our table on Mondays to accompany a big dish of boiled meats – bollito misto. But you can serve pepperonata with any meats, roast or boiled, or just on its own with fresh bread. Make sure to use the round bell peppers rather than the long thin Romano ones, as they are more meaty.

Michelle says: Delicious indeed on its own. If you don't want to serve it with gluten free bread, it is delicious with steamed new potatoes or rice, or quinoa grains cooked in gluten free vegetable stock.

SERVES 4

INGREDIENTS

2 lbs 4 oz/1kg large bell peppers, red, yellow and green

6 tbsp olive oil

2 onions, sliced

1 small fresh red chilli

2 garlic cloves, chopped

1 lb 8 oz/750g ripe tomatoes, peeled and roughly chopped

1 tbsp brown sugar

2 tbsp balsamic vinegar

1 oz/25g flat-leaf parsley leaves, chopped

sea salt and freshly ground black pepper

METHOD

Heat the oven to 350°F/180°C/Gas mark 4.

Wash and dry the peppers. Cut them vertically into half, then into quarters. Remove and discard the cores and seeds and cut them vertically into ½ inch/1 cm strips.

Heat the oil in a large sauté pan and when hot add the onions, with a large pinch of salt, to prevent them burning. Cook over a medium heat until soft. Stir frequently, so that the onion becomes soft and golden, but not brown.

Remove the seeds and core from the chilli, cut into very small pieces and add to the onions along with the garlic. Continue cooking for about a minute then add the peppers and continue to cook for 10 minutes over a lively heat, stirring frequently so that the peppers become well coated in oil.

Mix in the tomatoes with all their juices, bring the dish to a simmer and continue to cook for about 15 minutes to evaporate some of the liquid. Add the sugar and allow it to caramelise slightly while you stir gently, then add the vinegar. Mix well and season to taste.

Continue cooking for up to 45 minutes or until the peppers are soft. The peppers for pepperonata should be quite soft, not *al dente*. Sprinkle the dish with chopped flat-leaf arsley and serve hot, warm, or at room temperature.

POTATO AND ZUCCHINI/COURGETTE FRITTATA

Gluten free/can be milk-free/low lactose

Anna says: In Liguria, north-western Italy, vegetables are cooked in many different ways. Very often they are the main dish of the meal and this is a good example. You really cannot eat much else after this!

Michelle says: This dish has so much flavour anyhow that, if you want to go completely milk-free, you could leave out the Parmigiano-Reggiano or maybe add a few anchovies early on in the cooking. If you are on low lactose diet you should be fine with the Parmigiano-Reggiano as it is very low lactose.

SERVES 4 GENEROUSLY

INGREDIENTS

1lb/450g floury/starchy potatoes, all the same size

7 tbsp olive oil

1 medium onion, finely chopped

2 garlic cloves, finely chopped

1 lb 8 oz/700g zucchini/courgettes

1 oz/25g flat-leaf parsley leaves

4 eggs

5 tbsp freshly grated Parmigiano-Reggiano – or 4 anchovy fillets

2 tsp dried oregano

grating of nutmeg

dried, gluten free breadcrumbs

sea salt and freshly ground black pepper

METHOD

Scrub the potatoes and put them in a saucepan, cover with water and cook till tender. Drain them and peel them as soon as you can handle them. Pass them through a food mill, or a ricer, into a large bowl. Do not use the food processor as it will not aerate the potatoes, it will just make them gluey.

While the potatoes are cooking, heat 4 tablespoons of the oil in a large pan. Add the onion, garlic, 1 teaspoon of salt and the anchovies if you are using them, and sauté gently for 5 minutes, stirring regularly

Heat the oven to 350°F/180°C/Gas mark 4.

Wash and dry the zucchini/courgettes and cut them into thin rounds. Add them to the onion and garlic and sauté for around 5 minutes turning frequently so that all the rounds become covered in oil.

Add the parsley, 2–3 tablespoons of hot water and salt and pepper to taste. Cover the pan and continue cooking over a low heat for about 15 minutes or until the zucchini/courgettes are done. Do not forget to turn them over now and then. Add a little more water if they start to stick to the bottom of the pan. When they are done, scoop them with their juices into the bowl with the potatoes. Mix well.

Lightly beat the eggs together, mix in the Parmigiano-Reggiano (if you are using it), oregano, nutmeg and salt and pepper and then add this to the vegetables. Mix thoroughly.

Oil an ovenproof dish and lightly sprinkle with some of the gluten free breadcrumbs. Spoon in the potato and zucchini/courgette mixture and sprinkle more breadcrumbs over the top. Drizzle with the remaining oil.

Bake for 30 minutes. Remove to rest for a few minutes before serving hot, warm or at room temperature.

GRILLED RED RADICCHIO WITH ENDIVE/CHICORY

Gluten free/milk-free/lactose-free

Anna: The radicchio rosso used in the north-eastern Veneto region for this dish is the long radicchio of Treviso. You can sometimes find it in specialist greengrocers in the autumn. It has the characteristic bitterness of radicchio, delicate yet more pronounced than the more common, round, Rosa di Chioggia. This round radicchio is grown in greenhouses and is tougher in texture and blander in flavour.

Michelle: A super simple and totally free-from dish.

SERVES 4

INGREDIENTS

1 medium round red radicchio or 4 small/2 large, long radicchio

2 large or 4 small heads of endive/chicory

4–5 tbsp olive oil

sea salt and freshly ground black pepper

METHOD

Heat a grill/broiler or griddle.

Wash the vegetables carefully and dry thoroughly. Cut the vegetables in quarters or halves, depending on which you are using and the size.

Place the vegetables on a grill pan or griddle, spoon over the oil and season generously with salt and freshly ground black pepper.

Cook for 5 minutes, taking care the vegetables do not burn, then turn and cook for a further 5 minutes on the other side. The vegetables are ready when the thick core can be pierced easily.

Transfer the vegetables to a dish and spoon over the juices from the pan. Serve hot or cold.

SALADS

Bruschetta with tomatoes and mozzarella – **GF/MF/LF**

Carrot, celeriac and orange salad – **GF/MF/LF**

Cauliflower with anchovy and pine nuts – **GF/MF/LF**

Celeriac, endive/chicory and radicchio salad – **GF/MF/LF**

Fagiolini and tomato salad – **GF/MF/LF**

Pasta salad with sun-dried tomato sauce – **GF/can be MF/can be LF**

Warm salad of potatoes and green beans with pesto – **GF/MF/LF**

Tomatoes with buffalo mozzarella – **GF/CMF**

Tomato, cucumber and pepper salad – **GF/MF/LF**

Minty balsamic vinegar zucchini/courgette salad – **GF/MF/LF**

BRUSCHETTA WITH TOMATOES AND MOZZARELLA

Gluten free/milk-free/lactose-free

Anna says: Bruschetta is now common all over the world but to be good, it must be made with good tomatoes – ripe, sweet, yet full of flavour and with a thin skin as they must not be peeled. Plum tomatoes are particularly suitable as they do not have many seeds.

Michelle says: Bruschetta is traditionally made with ciabatta bread. It is possible to get gluten free versions of ciabatta which are moderately successful but if you cannot find one, it will still be worth making using a slice of a good, gluten free bread, brown or white, toasted. As Anna says, the important thing is the tomatoes.

SERVES 4

INGREDIENTS

6 good, ripe, thin-skinned tomatoes – plum tomatoes are ideal

sea salt

1 gluten free ciabatta or other gluten free rustic white loaf

2–3 garlic cloves cut into big pieces

2–3 tbsp extra virgin olive oil

freshly ground black pepper

12 basil leaves torn into large pieces

METHOD

Heat the oven to 375°F/190°C/Gas Mark 5.

Wash and dry the tomatoes. Cut them into small pieces, put on a wooden board and sprinkle with a little salt which will bring out the flavour. Leave for 30–40 minutes.

Cut the loaf into ½ inch/1.5 cm thick slices. Score the slices lightly with the point of a sharp knife and broil/grill on both sides – ideally over charcoal embers but under a broiler/grill will do fine. While it is still hot, rub with the garlic cloves. Put the slices in a hot oven for 2 minutes to crisp them through. Place on a dish, drizzle with olive oil and sprinkle generously with salt and pepper.

With a spoon, or slotted spoon, pick up the pieces of tomato leaving the juice behind and put them on the dressed bread.

Serve at once.

CARROT, CELERIAC AND ORANGE SALAD

Gluten free/milk-free/lactose-free

Anna says: Simple and tasty.

Michelle says: And free-from....

SERVES 4

INGREDIENTS

12 oz/350g carrots

6 oz/175g celeriac

2 oranges

juice ½ lemon

scant tsp gluten free French mustard

sea salt and freshly ground black pepper

3 tbsp extra virgin olive oil

METHOD

Peel and grate the carrots into a bowl. Peel the celeriac, discard any spongy flesh in the middle and grate into the bowl with the carrots.

Wash one of the oranges and dry it. Grate the rind from half of it into a separate bowl. Squeeze the juice from the grated half of the orange in with the rind and add the lemon juice, mustard, salt and pepper.

Whisk and continue to whisk while gradually adding the oil. Taste and add more orange or lemon juice and seasoning to taste. Spoon over the vegetables, mix thoroughly and pile onto a dish.

Peel the remaining whole and half oranges and slice them. Place them round the vegetables. Cover and leave for 30 minutes before eating.

CAULIFLOWER SALAD WITH ANCHOVY AND PINE NUT DRESSING

Gluten free/milk-free/lactose-free

Anna says: I have adapted this recipe from an 18th century Neapolitan cookery writer, Vincenzo Corrado. Cauliflower and anchovy have always been a successful combination.

Michelle says: As Anna says, cauliflower and anchovy go brilliantly together – and make a great free-from salad.

SERVES 4

INGREDIENTS

1 medium to large head of cauliflower

4 tbsp extra virgin olive oil

2 oz/50g pine nuts

8 canned anchovy fillets

1 tbsp white wine vinegar

1 tbsp lemon juice

sea salt and freshly ground black pepper

2 tbsp chopped parsley

METHOD

Divide the cauliflower into small florets. Wash them thoroughly then cook in plenty of well salted water until tender. As an Italian, I like my vegetables properly cooked – in other words they should be tender when pricked with a fork but not soft, as it is at that stage that they develop their full flavour. This does not happen if they are served semi-raw!

Dry the florets thoroughly with kitchen paper and toss them gently in 1–2 tablespoons of the oil while they are still warm so that they absorb the flavour.

Dry roast the pine nuts for a few minutes in a non-stick pan to bring out the flavour.

Drain the anchovy fillets and put them with the vinegar, lemon juice, salt and pepper, in a pestle and mortar or a food processor. Pound with the pestle or process then drizzle in the rest of the oil to make an emulsion.

Spoon the sauce over the cauliflower, cover and leave for an hour.

To serve, sprinkle with the chopped parsley and serve at room temperature with crusty, gluten free bread.

CELERIAC, ENDIVE/CHICORY AND RADICCHIO SALAD

Gluten free/milk-free/lactose-free

Anna says: An autumnal salad, full of colours and flavours.

Michelle says: Remember to check the mustard powder to make sure that it is gluten free; some contain thickeners.

SERVES 4

INGREDIENTS

1–2 tbsp lemon juice, depending on how lemony you like your dressings

½ tsp gluten free, English mustard powder

3 tbsp extra virgin olive oil

½ medium sized celeriac bulb

2 small/1 large head of endive/chicory

1 small head radicchio

METHOD

First make the dressing. Put the lemon juice in a bowl and mix in the mustard powder. Add the oil in a very thin stream while beating with a fork or small whisk to emulsify. Then season to taste.

Peel the celeriac and cut into julienne strips in a food processor or grate. Toss with some of the dressing and put into a bowl. Cover and set aside for 2–3 hours.

Cut the chicory and radicchio into ½ inch/1 cm strips. Wash and dry them thoroughly then toss in the remaining dressing.

Put the celeriac in the middle of a dish and spoon the salad mixture around it.

FAGIOLINI AND TOMATO SALAD

Gluten free/milk-free/lactose-free

Anna says: The beans can be prepared well in advance and stored in the refrigerator; the tomatoes can be prepared several hours in advance but only dress the salad just before serving it.

Michelle says: Lovely gluten free Italian salad.

SERVES 4

INGREDIENTS

1 lb/450g green/French beans

sea salt

4 tbsp extra virgin olive oil

8 oz/225g firm, ripe tomatoes

3 garlic cloves, bruised

1 tbsp lemon juice

freshly ground black pepper

6 fresh basil leaves

METHOD

Top and tail the beans and cook, uncovered, in plenty of very well salted water until *al dente*. Drain and refresh quickly under cold water. Dry with kitchen paper then heap them in the middle of a dish and dress with a generous tablespoon of olive oil while they are still warm.

While the beans are cooking, drop the tomatoes into the cooking water and count to eight. Remove them with a slotted spoon and plunge immediately into cold water. Skin them and cut into wedges or slices, discarding the seeds.

Put the rest of the oil, the garlic, lemon juice and plenty of pepper into a bowl and leave to infuse for at least an hour. Then, remove the garlic.

Lay the tomatoes around the beans on the dish and spoon the dressing over both. Scatter over the basil leaves and serve at once.

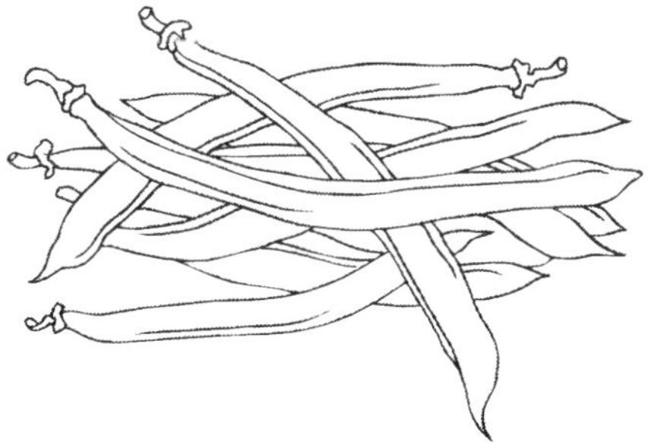

PASTA SALAD WITH SUN-DRIED TOMATO SAUCE

Gluten free/can be milk-free/can be lactose-free

Anna says: I am not particularly keen on pasta salad but and this sun-dried tomato sauce is particularly good for cold pasta and works very well with gluten free pasta. I suggest one teaspoon of crushed chilli, but of course, you can use less if you want to spare your palate from strong shocks (or more if you want to set your mouth on fire). Use plain olives, not the sort dressed with different flavours.

Michelle says: Great flavour and very easy to make milk-free as well as gluten free.

SERVES 4

INGREDIENTS

5 oz/125g dry sun-dried tomatoes (not in oil)

1 tbsp red wine vinegar

1 tbsp balsamic vinegar

sea salt

8 tbsp extra virgin olive oil

1 tsp crushed chilli

3 garlic cloves, peeled and chopped

1 tbsp dried oregano

2 tbsp tomato pesto, or if you want the dish to be milk-free, milk-free tomato pesto

400g gluten free spaghetti

12 pitted black olives

METHOD

Put the tomatoes in a bowl, pour over the red wine vinegar and balsamic vinegar, sprinkle with a pinch or two of salt and leave them to reconstitute for at least 1 hour.

Drain the tomatoes, dry them with kitchen paper and chop them coarsely. Put them into a bowl and add 6 tablespoons of the olive oil, the chilli, garlic, ½ tablespoon of the oregano and the pesto. Mix well and set aside while you cook the pasta.

Cook the pasta in well salted water, according to the instructions on the pack. Drain and turn immediately into the bowl with the tomatoes. Mix well and leave the pasta to cool. Do not refrigerate because the salad should be served at room temperature.

Before serving, scatter the olives over the top, shower with the remaining ½ tablespoon of oregano, and pour over the remaining 2 tablespoons of olive oil.

WARM SALAD OF POTATOES AND GREEN BEANS WITH PESTO

Gluten free/milk-free/lactose-free

Anna says: In Genoa, pasta al pesto often contains potatoes and green beans. Here I have eliminated the pasta and just serve the beans and potatoes as a delicious warm salad.

Michelle says: Surprisingly, pasta and potatoes work very well together – but Anna's salad is already filling enough without the pasta!

SERVES 4

INGREDIENTS

2 oz/50g fresh basil leaves

2 garlic cloves, peeled

1 oz/25g pine nuts

sea salt and freshly ground black pepper

2 tbsp extra virgin olive oil

1 lb 8 oz/750g new potatoes, all the same size

1 lb/450g French/ green beans/ fagiolini

3 tbsp extra virgin olive oil

sea salt

METHOD

First make the pesto. These amounts will probably make more pesto than you need for this dish, so can be used in another dish – or just on toast or as a dip. It will keep in the fridge for 2–3 days.

Put all basil leaves, garlic, pine nuts, salt, pepper and the 2 tablespoons of olive oil into a food processor and whizz until completely blended. Taste and check the seasonings.

Boil the potatoes in their skins. When cooked, drain and peel them while still hot. Leave aside.

Top and tail the beans and cook them in well salted water until tender but not soft – a sharp knife should go through them easily and they will still be a lovely green colour. Drain and dry them and cut into 1 inch/2.5cm lengths.

While the beans are cooking, cut the potatoes into ¾ inch/2cm cubes, put them in a bowl and dress with olive oil.

Add the beans to the potatoes, spoon at least half the pesto into the salad and toss gently – add extra pesto if you think it needs more and serve warm.

TOMATOES WITH BUFFALO MOZZARELLA

Gluten free/cow's milk-free

Anna says: This is the simplest and best antipasto, but you must not try to make it unless you have very good tomatoes – tasty and juicy, not woolly and dry. The best round tomatoes come from Calabria or Campania and are sold still attached to their stems. Also, be sure to use buffalo mozzarella which has a much deeper flavour than cow's milk mozzarella.

Michelle says: You cannot make this dish without mozzarella but, as Anna says, buffalo mozzarella has a much better flavour than cow's and many people who cannot tolerate cow's milk get on just fine with buffalo milk.

SERVES 4

INGREDIENTS

12 ripe tomatoes

sea salt and freshly ground black pepper

12 oz/350g buffalo mozzarella

6 tbsp extra virgin olive oil

24 fresh basil leaves

METHOD

Wash and dry the tomatoes and cut them in half. Squeeze out a little of the juice and sprinkle with salt. Lay the tomato halves on a wooden board, cut side down and set aside for at least 30 minutes.

Wipe the inside of the tomatoes with kitchen paper and place, cut side up, on a dish.

Cut the mozzarella into 24 slices or pieces and put one piece inside each tomato half. Season with a generous grind of pepper and drizzle over a little olive oil.

Wipe the basil leaves with a moistened piece of kitchen paper and place a leaf over each piece of mozzarella.

Serve at once.

TOMATO, CUCUMBER AND PEPPER SALAD

Gluten free/milk-free/lactose-free

Anna says: I do not like raw onions. They are too overwhelming and kill the flavours of the other ingredients. So, if you are like me you must start this very traditional Italian dish a day in advance.

Michelle says: Marinating the onions gives this dish a whole other perspective – try it!

SERVES 4

INGREDIENTS

1 large or 2 small red onions

juice of 2 organic lemons

1 tsp superfine/caster sugar

½ large cucumber

2 large or 4 medium-sized tomatoes

2 large bell peppers, one red one yellow

4 tbsp extra virgin olive oil

ground black pepper

METHOD

Peel the onions and slice very finely. Put them in a bowl, add 4 tablespoons of the lemon juice and the sugar. Mix well, cover and leave overnight.

Peel the cucumber and slice it thinly. Put the slices in a bowl, sprinkle with salt, cover and leave for an hour.

Wash and dry the tomatoes. Slice them very thinly and put them in a salad bowl.

Wash and dry the peppers. Deseed them and cut them into thin strips. Add to the bowl.

Squeeze the liquid out of the cucumber and add the slices to the bowl. Then do the same with the onion.

Just before serving, toss the salad with the olive oil and most of the remaining lemon juice. Season with a generous amount of black pepper and salt to taste. Add more lemon if necessary – and serve.

MINTY BALSAMIC VINEGAR ZUCCHINI/COURGETTE SALAD

Gluten free/milk-free/lactose-free

Anna says: A classic Italian dish given an unusual twist with the balsamic and the addition of mint.

Michelle says: The fresh mint is a brilliant addition.

SERVES 4

INGREDIENTS

1 lb/225g young zucchini/courgettes

sea salt

3 tbsp extra virgin olive oil

1½ tbsp balsamic vinegar

freshly ground black pepper

1 small garlic clove, finely sliced

2 large or 4 small plum tomatoes

1½ tbsp chopped fresh mint, reserving a few leaves

METHOD

Wash the zucchini/courgettes thoroughly, leaving the end on to prevent water from getting inside. Cook in boiling, salted water until just tender (a sharp knife goes in easily) but not soft.

Take them out of the saucepan and refresh them in cold water. Allow to cool slightly.

Cut off the end and slice in half lengthways. Lay them on a dish cut side upwards.

Mix together the oil, balsamic, pepper and salt and spoon over the zucchini/ courgettes, reserving 1 tablespoon of the dressing. Sprinkle the garlic slivers on top, cover and set aside for 1 hour.

Blanch and skin the tomatoes. Cut them in half and squeeze out and discard the seeds and some of the liquid. Cut them into ½ inch/1 cm cubes and put them into a bowl. Season with salt and pepper and toss with the remaining dressing. Spoon the mixture over the zucchini halves and sprinkle the fresh mint leaves here and there over the top.

ALBERTO ARRIZZI

DESSERTS & CAKES

Sautéed sliced apples with Calvados – **GF/can be MF/can be LF**

Plums in wine syrup – **GF/MF/LF**

Pears in red wine with liqueur cream – **GF/can be MF/can be LF**

Strawberries or melon with balsamic vinegar – **GF/LF/MF**

Coffee flavoured Panna Cotta – **GF/can be MF/can be LF**

Francesca's chocolate mousse – **GF/MF/LF**

Chocolate and hazelnut truffle cups – **GF/can be MF/can be LF**

Strawberry ice cream with balsamic – **GF/can be MF/can be LF**

Basil and lemon sorbet – **GF/MF/LF**

Carrot, almond and rum cake – **GF/MF/LF**

Castagnaccio – Chestnut flour cake – **GF/MF/LF**

Buckwheat cake – **GF/can be MF/can be LF**

SAUTÉED, SLICED APPLES WITH CALVADOS

Gluten free/can be milk-free/can be lactose-free

Anna says: This recipe has a noble pedigree being based, we think, on a recipe of the great Bartolomeo Stefani, chef to the Gonzaga family in the mid 17th century. You can serve some cream with it, although personally, I prefer it without.

Michelle says: Anna would rightly say that the flavour of the butter in this dish is one of its glories but.... If you cannot eat butter, you could actually make it with a dairy-free spread. There are so many other delicious flavours in the dish that even though it may not be quite as wonderful as the original, it is still pretty delicious.

SERVES 4

INGREDIENTS

4 crisp dessert apples

2 oz/50g unsalted butter or dairy-free spread

4–5 oz/120g–150g superfine/caster sugar

2 organic unwaxed lemons

4 tbsp fresh orange juice

4 tbsp Calvados

METHOD

Peel the apples and remove the core, leaving the apples whole. Cut them horizontally into slices approximately ½ inch/1 cm thick.

Choose a large frying pan into which the apple slices will fit in a single layer. If you do not have a big enough one, use two pans, increasing the amount of butter/spread slightly.

Put the butter in the pan and, when soft, add 3–4 tablespoons of the sugar and cook until the sugar has slightly caramelised. Lay the apple slices over the caramelised sugar and cook briskly until golden. Gently turn the slices over, add another couple of tablespoons of sugar and cook until this side is golden too. Turn the heat down low.

Wash one of the lemons, grate the rind and add to the pan. Squeeze both lemons and add 6 tablespoons of the juice to the pan along with the orange juice.

Continue cooking, while gradually adding the rest of the sugar, until the apples can easily be pierced with a sharp knife.

Heat the Calvados in a metal ladle then pour it into the pan while you put a match to it.

Let the flames die down. Spoon the juices over each helping and serve at once.

PLUMS IN WINE SYRUP

Gluten free/milk-free/lactose-free

Anna says: Adding rosemary to stewing plums was one of those happy accidents that turned out really well. The rosemary is hardly detectable, yet it gives the juice of the fruit a certain *je ne sais quoi* which never fails to puzzle people.

Michelle says: A happy mistake indeed. And naturally gluten and milk-free.

SERVES 4

INGREDIENTS

1 cup/8fl oz/250ml good red wine

6 oz/150g superfine/caster sugar

1 generous sprig of fresh rosemary

1 strip organic lemon rind with no pith

2 cloves

1 cinnamon stick

4 peppercorns, bruised

1 lb 8 oz/750g plums, ripe but firm, washed

METHOD

Put all the ingredients, apart from the plums, into a wide saucepan big enough to hold the plums in a single layer. Pour over 1 cup/8fl oz/250ml water.

Heat gently, stirring with a wooden spoon, until the sugar has dissolved. Lay the plums over the melted sugar, cover the pan and cook gently until the plums are soft but still whole. Transfer the plums with a slotted spoon to a bowl.

Strain the syrup into a clean pan and boil rapidly, uncovered, until thick and syrupy.

Pour the syrup over the plums. Cover and refrigerate before serving.

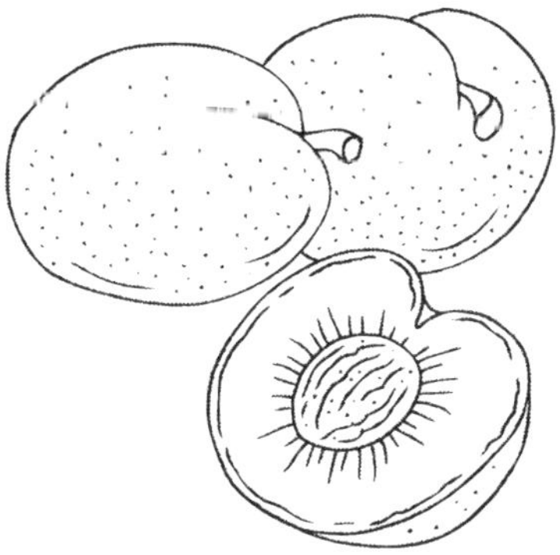

PEARS IN RED WINE WITH LIQUEUR CREAM

Gluten free/can be milk-free/can be lactose-free

Anna says: The pears make a very good foil for this delicious syllabub.

Michelle says: Although, once again Anna will not approve, you can make the syllabub with a coconut or soya yogurt. The flavour will obviously be somewhat different and it will be slightly softer but that does not mean that it will not be very tasty!

SERVES 4

INGREDIENTS

2 ripe but firm pears

grated rind and juice of ½ an organic lemon

6 oz/150g superfine/caster sugar

1 cinnamon stick

1 cup/8fl oz/250ml good red wine

2 tbsp Poire William Eau de Vie or Italian Grappa alla Pera

1 ¼ cups/10fl oz/300ml whipping cream, or stiff coconut or soya yogurt

METHOD

Peel the pears, cut them into quarters and remove the core. As you peel them, drop them into a bowl of cold water containing the juice of ¼ of a lemon to prevent them discolouring.

Put half the sugar, the cinnamon stick and the wine into a saucepan and heat gently until the sugar has dissolved. Add the pears and cook until tender – 10–15 minutes. Lift them out of the liquid and set aside.

While the pears are cooling, add the remaining sugar, lemon rind and juice and the liqueur, and cook gently until the sugar has dissolved.

Whip the cream until it stands in soft peaks then slowly fold it into the liqueur mixture. (If you are using the coconut yoghurt, just fold in the liqueur mixture.)

Lift the pears out of the syrup (you can use it to flavour a fruit salad) and place two quarters in each dish. Spoon over the cream and chill for at least an hour before serving.

STRAWBERRIES OR MELON WITH BALSAMIC VINEGAR

Gluten free/milk-free/lactose-free

Anna says: A very simple but delicious way to bring out the flavour of both the strawberries and the melon. The most popular melon in Italy is the cantaloupe but the recipe works well with any melon.

Michelle says: Although Anna specifies strawberries or melon, you can give virtually any soft fruit this treatment and it will work well.

SERVES 4

INGREDIENTS

1 lb 8 oz/750g strawberries, hulled, or
1 medium size melon

1–3 tbsp superfine/caster sugar, depending on the sweetness of the fruit. NB: Provided it is ripe, you will need less sugar for the melon than for the strawberries.

2 tbsp best quality balsamic vinegar

METHOD

If you are using strawberries, cut them into or quarters, depending on their size.

Put the strawberries into an attractive bowl, preferably a glass one.

About 2 hours before serving sprinkle over half of the sugar and toss gently but thoroughly. Half an hour before serving sprinkle the rest of the sugar over the strawberries. Drizzle over the balsamic and toss with care. Refrigerate.

If you are using melon, remove the skin and cut it into suitable small bits. Sprinkle with the sugar, drizzle over the balsamic and toss with care. Put in the fridge for half an hour and then serve.

Serve both fruits chilled.

COFFEE FLAVOURED PANNA COTTA

Gluten free/can be milk-free/can be lactose-free

Anna says: I am a purist and a traditionalist so I really prefer my panna cotta served entirely unflavoured and by itself so that you can appreciate the quality of the cream. However, even I have to admit that this coffee flavoured version is really good. The secret of a good panna cotta is to use just enough gelatine for it to set but not enough to make it firm – it should be wobbly and trembly. If you can find it, I think that leaf gelatine works better than powdered.

Michelle says: Although Anna shudders at the very suggestion, I have made very successful panna cotta with alternative milks. I used coconut but if you really dislike the flavour of coconut you could use almond (very Italian) or even soya, although I am not sure that soya works so well for desserts and sweet dishes.

SERVES 4–6, DEPENDING ON THE SIZE OF YOUR RAMEKIN DISHES.

INGREDIENTS

⅓ oz/10g gelatine leaves or 2 tsp unflavoured gelatine powder
NB: If you are using an alternative milk you will need to use a little extra gelatine as they are thinner than heavy cream.
I would suggest ½ oz/15g gelatine leaves, or 2 heaped tsp gelatine powder

2 cups/16fl oz/450ml heavy/double cream

5fl oz/150ml full fat/whole milk
or for the milk-free version 2½ cups/12fl oz/370ml coconut milk or almond milk

4 oz/100g superfine/caster sugar

2 tsp instant expresso coffee powder

½ tsp pure vanilla extract

4 tbsp dark rum

2–3 oz/50–75g chocolate covered coffee beans for decoration

METHOD

If you are using gelatine leaves, put them in a bowl and fill with water. As soon as they are soft enough, bend them so they are submerged and leave for 15 minutes. Squeeze the leaves out and put in a saucepan with 4 tablespoons of water. Heat slowly, stirring constantly until they have dissolved.

If using powdered gelatine, put 4 tbsp water in a small pan and sprinkle over the gelatine. Allow to soak for 10 minutes then very gradually heat until the powder is dissolved. Take care not to boil.

If you are using cream and milk, mix them together in a saucepan. Add the sugar, and heat gently until the sugar has dissolved. Stir in the coffee powder and the vanilla.

If you are using alternative milks, add the sugar and heat gently until the gelatine has dissolved. Then, add the coffee powder and vanilla.

Draw off the heat and add the rum and the gelatine. Mix thoroughly. Cool in the fridge for 1 hour.

To serve, run a knife, previously dipped in boiling water, around each ramekin and unmould the panna cotta onto individual serving plates. Decorate each with the dairy-free chocolate covered coffee beans.

FRANCESCA'S CHOCOLATE MOUSSE

Gluten free/milk-free/lactose-free

Anna says: A very easy recipe which I used when making chocolate pudding with my grandchildren. They could make the pudding all by themselves – no cooking involved – and loved the result.

Michelle says: And naturally gluten and dairy-free too...

MAKES 4 SMALL POTS

INGREDIENTS

3 eggs, separated

3 tbsp superfine/caster sugar

4 oz/100g dark (minimum 70%), milk-free chocolate

candied violets to decorate (optional)

METHOD

Separate the eggs and whisk the egg whites until they form soft peaks.

In a separate bowl, beat the egg yolks with the sugar, until pale.

Break the chocolate into little pieces and melt it in a bowl over simmering hot water, or, in a microwave. Mix the chocolate into the egg yolks and sugar and then fold in the egg whites keeping as much air in the white as possible as you do so. Spoon the mousse into 4 pots or ramekins.

My grandchildren used to decorate the mousses with candied violets, but you could also use an almond or just some grated chocolate.

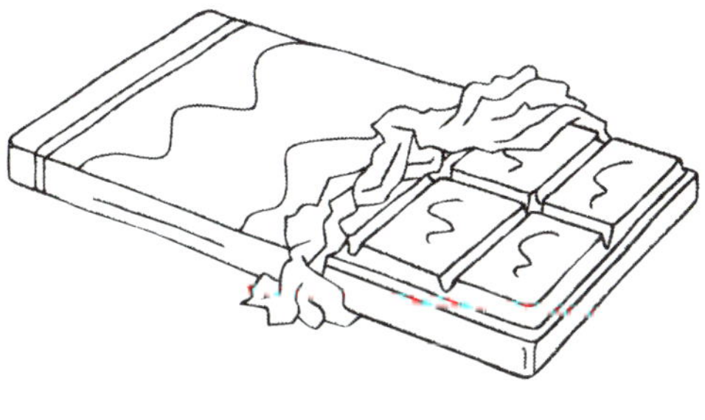

CHOCOLATE AND HAZELNUT TRUFFLE CUPS

Gluten free/can be milk-free/can be lactose-free

Anna says: This recipe is based on one in Maddalena Bonino's lovely book *Fast and Fresh Entertaining*. The flavours remind me of the delicious Gianduiotti, the Torinese chocolates, traditionally wrapped in gold paper and made from a mixture of chocolate and hazelnuts.

Michelle says: If you want to avoid milk you can substitute a thick coconut, almond or soya yogurt for the cream. It will obviously slightly change the flavour of the dish and the texture will be somewhat softer, but it will still be delicious.

SERVES 4

INGREDIENTS

6 oz/170g dark, dairy-free, minimum 70% cocoa solids chocolate

2–3 tbsp rum or brandy

4 oz/100g hazelnuts, lightly toasted, skins removed and roughly chopped

2 egg whites

1–2 tbsp superfine/caster sugar, depending on how sweet you want it to be

1 ¼ cups/10fl oz/300ml heavy/double cream or thick coconut, almond or soya yogurt

METHOD

Melt the chocolate with the rum or brandy and the hazelnuts, in a bowl over simmering hot water or in a microwave. When melted, remove and cool, stirring occasionally, until lukewarm.

Whisk the egg whites until stiff then add the sugar and whisk again still stiff. Fold into the chocolate mixture.

If you are using it, whisk the cream until thick. Fold it or the coconut, almond or soya yogurt into the chocolate mixture and taste for sweetness. If needed, add a little extra sugar.

Spoon into glasses or small bowl and chill for at least 1 hour before serving.

STRAWBERRY ICE CREAM WITH BALSAMIC VINEGAR

Gluten free/can be milk-free/can be lactose-free

Anna says: This is one of my best original recipes as the balsamic vinegar brings out the flavour and aroma of the strawberries so intensely. As with all fruit ice creams it is better eaten within a day of making.

Michelle says: Anna makes her ice cream with whipping cream but if you want it to be milk-free, it also works well with a coconut or a soya cream or yogurt.

SERVES 4 GENEROUSLY

INGREDIENTS

1 lb/450g strawberries

5 oz/150g superfine/caster sugar

1 tbsp good balsamic vinegar

⅔ cup/5fl oz/150ml whipping cream or coconut yogurt or soya cream

METHOD

Wash and hull the strawberries. Dry them with kitchen towel and put them into a food processor with the sugar. Start the processor and add the balsamic gradually through the funnel.

Transfer the mixture to a bowl and refrigerate for 2–3 hours.

Whip the cream to soft peaks then fold in the strawberry mixture, or, if you are not using the cream, fold the strawberry mixture into the coconut/soya yogurt or cream.

Transfer to an ice cream maker if you have one and freeze. If you don't have an ice cream maker, freeze in a bowl, preferably metal, but remove it from the freezer and stir vigorously two or three times during the freezing process to break up the ice crystals. This will achieve a relatively smooth texture.

Remove from the freezer and place in the fridge half an hour before serving.

BASIL AND LEMON SORBET

Gluten free/milk-free/lactose-free

Anna says: The basil-flavour in this sorbet is not immediately identifiable but it transforms an everyday lemon sorbet into a conversation stopper. However, be sure to use young basil leaves as old leaves have a strong, minty flavour, which is wrong for this dish.

Michelle says: Yum...

SERVES 4–6

INGREDIENTS

8 organic lemons

2 organic oranges

2 ¼ cups/1pint/600ml water

12 oz/300g superfine/caster sugar

24 large young basil leaves, chopped

METHOD

Wash the fruit and remove the rind, without chipping into the white pith. Put in a saucepan.

Add the water and sugar, bring to the boil and simmer until the sugar has dissolved.

Turn the heat up to moderate and boil rapidly for 3 minutes. Draw off the heat, allow to cool completely then strain and discard the rind.

Meanwhile, squeeze the lemons and oranges – you should get around 2 cups/16fl oz/500ml – and add to the cold syrup with the basil leaves.

If you have an ice cream maker, pour in the mixture and churn freeze.

If you don't have an ice cream make, freeze in a metal bowl, if you have one, for about 2 hours or until it is half frozen. Remove from the fridge and put in the sink (to stop it splattering everywhere) and then beat with a hand electric beater or whisk to break down the ice crystals. Return to the freezer and repeat the process an hour later.

Remove from the freezer and place in the fridge half an hour before eating. Eat within 24 hours as fruit sorbets lose their flavour very quickly.

CARROT, ALMOND AND RUM CAKE

Gluten free/milk-free/lactose-free

Anna says: This is a very good cake, the fragrant freshness of the almond acquires a deeper side through the darker flavour of the carrot and the rum. As with most country cakes, the finishing is simply a thick layer of icing sugar.

Michelle says: This is indeed a very good cake – and it is naturally both gluten and milk-free! If you wanted to serve it as a dessert you could do so with a fruit coulis.

INGREDIENTS

5 oz/150 shelled almonds

5 oz/150g carrots, finely grated

3 eggs, separated

4 oz/100g soft brown/muscovado sugar

2 oz/60g potato flour

sea salt

1 ½ level tsp gluten free baking powder

2 tbsp rum

confectioner's/icing sugar

METHOD

Heat the oven to 350°F/180°C/Gas mark 4.

Spread the almonds onto a baking tray and place the tray in the oven for 7–8 minutes. This will bring their flavour out.

Chop the almonds in a food processor, or by hand, until they are like very small grains.

Peel and grate the carrots.

Beat the egg yolks with the sugar, until pale and holding their shape. Sift the potato flour with the salt and baking powder and add it, with a large metal spoon, to the egg and sugar mixture. Fold in well then add the carrots and rum. Mix thoroughly.

Whisk the egg whites until standing in firm peaks. Fold them gradually and carefully into the carrot mixture.

Oil a loose-bottomed, 7 inch/18cm tin, or line a tin with oiled greaseproof paper/ baking parchment. Spoon the cake mixture into the tin and bake for 40–45 minutes or until a skewer comes out clean and the cake is a lovely golden colour. It should have shrunk slightly from the sides of the tin.

Allow to cool for 15 minutes. Remove from the tin and turn onto a wire rack. Cool completely and then shower with sieved icing sugar.

CASTAGNACCIO - CHESTNUT FLOUR CAKE

Gluten free/milk-free/lactose-free

Anna says: In Lucca, in Tuscany, where this recipe originates, slices of castagnaccio, or chestnut flour cake are sold in bakers' shops and eaten in the streets. Because chestnut flour goes stale quickly, keep it in the freezer until you want to use it.

Michelle says: Another great naturally gluten and milk-free cake. You can usually buy chestnut flour in Italian delis, in health food stores or online.

INGREDIENTS

2½ oz/60g golden raisins/sultanas

10 oz/300g chestnut flour

pinch salt

2 tbsp superfine/caster sugar

3 tbsp extra virgin olive oil

2 oz/50g pine nuts

1 tbsp fresh rosemary needles

21 cm x 11 cm loaf tin

METHOD

Soak the golden raisins/sultanas in warm water for 20 minutes.

Heat the oven to 400°F/200°C/Gas mark 6.

Sift the chestnut flour into a bowl and add 1¾ cups/14fl oz/400ml cold water, to make a smooth, soft batter. Add 2 tablespoons of oil and the sultanas and stir well.

Line and grease a cake tin with oil. The tin, which traditionally should be rectangular, must be large enough to allow the mixture to spread to a thickness of about ¾ inch/2cm.

Pour in the chestnut batter and sprinkle the top with pine nuts and rosemary needles. Dribble over the rest of the oil.

Bake for 35–40 minutes until the top is crisp and cracked and a lovely deep brown in colour.

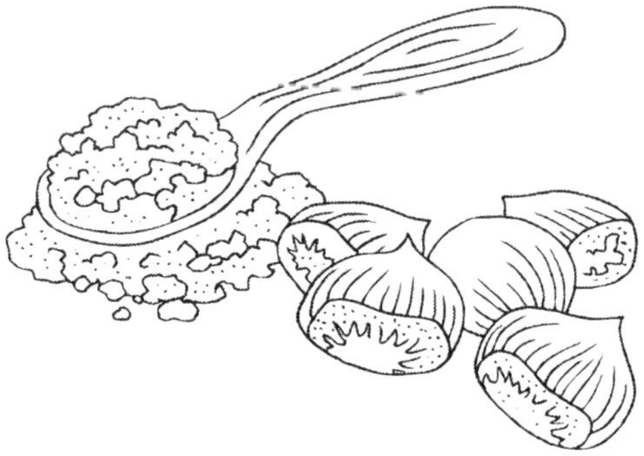

BUCKWHEAT CAKE

Gluten free/can be milk-free/can be lactose-free

Anna says: This recipe came originally from the Pasticceria Konig in the town of Merano, in the South Tyrol, northern Italy. It is famous for its wonderful cakes and buckwheat is grown locally. For the cake to be at its best, the almonds must be very fresh.

Michelle says: Buckwheat is, despite its name, naturally gluten free and all you need to do to make this delicious cake milk-free as well is to substitute a milk-free spread for the butter.

INGREDIENTS

4 oz/125g shelled almonds, skin on (you could use ground almonds, but the flavour won't be as good)

5 oz/125g superfine/caster sugar

5 oz/125g soft butter or dairy-free spread

3 large eggs, separated

5 oz/125g fine buckwheat flour

2 tsp gluten free baking powder

pinch salt

1 tsp grated lemon rind from an unwaxed lemon

2 pinches ground cinnamon

butter, dairy-free spread or oil for the tin

approx. 12 oz/350g best blackcurrant jam

confectioner's/icing sugar to decorate

METHOD

Heat the oven to 350°F/180°C/Gas mark 4.

Blanch half the almonds in boiling water for 30 seconds. Drain and skin them by squeezing the almond out of its skin between your thumb and index finger. Spread the skinned almonds, and those in their skins on a baking tray and toast them for 10 minutes to release the flavour. Allow to cool then grind finely in a food processor to a small grainy texture.

Beat 3 oz/75g of the sugar with the butter/spread, until light and creamy. Incorporate the egg yolks thoroughly into the mixture then add the buckwheat flour, baking powder, lemon rind, almonds and cinnamon. Mix thoroughly.

Whisk the egg whites until soft peaks form. Whisk in half the remaining sugar by the tablespoon and then finally fold in the rest of the sugar. Fold the meringue into the buckwheat mixture using a metal spoon with a gentle but deep movement.

Line, and then butter or oil an 8 inch/20cm, loose-bottomed cake tin or spring-clip tin and then spoon in the cake mixture. Bake for 30–40 minutes, or until a skewer inserted into the middle of the cake comes out clean. Allow to cool and when still just warm carefully unmould onto a rack – carefully, because this is quite a fragile cake!

When cool use a sharp or serrated knife to cut the cake in half to form two flat rounds. Spread the jam generously over the bottom round them replace the top one and sprinkle lavishly with confectioner's/icing sugar.

RECIPE INDEX

Q

R

Printed in Great Britain
by Amazon

43194147R00121